Branding & Networking Success for Bands

Neil J Milliner

Published by Neil Milliner, 2024.

While every precaution has been taken in the preparation of this book, the publisher assumes no responsibility for errors or omissions, or for damages resulting from the use of the information contained herein.

BRANDING & NETWORKING SUCCESS FOR BANDS

First edition. October 20, 2024.

Copyright © 2024 Neil J Milliner.

ISBN: 979-8227512901

Written by Neil J Milliner.

Also by Neil J Milliner

Artful Investments: Enhancing Your Property Value Through Fine Art
E-commerce SEO Strategies: Selling Online Successfully
Fast Track Your Songwriting Career-Essential Tips and Hints to Master Your Craft and Build a Lasting Career
The Ultimate Singer's Guide-Practical Tips to Improve Your Voice and Achieve Your Vocal Dreams
Branding & Networking Success for Bands
Mastering Fan Engagement-Pro-Level Hints to Create Authentic Connections and Build Loyalty
Mastering Live Performance & Touring-Pro Level Tips and Hints to Elevate Your Stage Presence and Tour Like a Pro
Music Production Mastery-Step-by-Step Tutorials to Fast-Track Your Way to Professional Success
The Musician's Tech Toolbox-Essential Technical Tips and Equipment Know-How for Musicians
The Ultimate Musician's Website Guide-Step-by-Step Tutorials to Engage Fans and Showcase Your Talent

Contents

How to Effectively Market Yourself as a Musician by Telling Your Authentic Story

Boost Your Social Media Presence with Smart Hashtags: Effective Hashtag Strategies

Strategies for Getting Featured on Spotify Playlists

Boost Your Music Video Views with YouTube Optimization

Creating Engaging Visual Content: Design Tips

Tips for Starting and Sustaining Your Music Blog

Effective Networking Techniques for Introverts

Developing Your Music Brand: A Step-by-Step Guide

Designing and Selling Merch That Sells

Fan Demographics: Analyzing Data for Targeted Marketing

Music Video Storyboarding: Solving Visual Narrative Challenges

Effective Press Releases: Crafting Newsworthy Announcements

Creating Engaging Content: Storytelling for Music Blogs

Best Practices for Booking Gigs Successfully

Fan Engagement Strategies for Authentic Connection

Effective Band Bios: Crafting Compelling Artist Stories

Success With Music Collaboration: Overcoming Communication Challenges

Fan Feedback: Handling Criticism and Building Resilience

Tips to Enhance Content Virality

Creating Engaging Instagram Stories: Troubleshooting Tips & Optimization Strategies

Building Your Email Fanbase: Effective Email Marketing Strategies to Engage Your Audience

Creating a Killer EPK: Essential Elements and Troubleshooting

Live Streaming Hacks: Troubleshooting Livestream Issues

SEO for Musicians: Boosting Website Visibility and Optimizing for Search Engines

Social Media Algorithms Decoded: Understanding and Maximizing Your Reach
Expand Your Email Subscriber List Cost-Free
Uncover 7 Free Strategies to Boost Website Traffic
Website Loading Woes: Speed Optimization for Musicians
DIY Music Videos: Solving Lighting and Filming Challenges

How to Effectively Market Yourself as a Musician by Telling Your Authentic Story

In today's crowded music industry, where countless artists are competing for attention, your music alone may not be enough to stand out. One of the most powerful ways to differentiate yourself is by telling your authentic story. Sharing your personal journey, struggles, and triumphs helps you connect with your audience on a deeper level. In this blog post, we'll explore how to effectively market yourself as a musician by tapping into the power of storytelling.

1. Embrace Vulnerability in Your Story

ONE OF THE KEY ELEMENTS of an authentic story is vulnerability. Sharing your personal experiences, struggles, and the obstacles you've overcome humanizes you and makes it easier for your audience to relate to you. When people see your authentic self, they're more likely to form a deeper connection with your music.

How to Do It:

- Share your journey honestly: Whether you've struggled with stage fright, financial hardship, or creative blocks, opening up about these challenges makes your story more relatable.

- Highlight defining moments: Was there a pivotal moment when you decided to pursue music full-time, or a life event that shaped your sound? Share these moments to add depth to your narrative.

- Be true to your personality: Don't try to craft a persona you think people will like. Authenticity shines through when you embrace who you truly are.

2. Identify the Themes in Your Story

YOUR LIFE AS A MUSICIAN may have different layers, such as your background, the experiences that shaped you, and the message you want to convey through your music. Identifying the central themes in your story helps you create a cohesive narrative that resonates with your audience.

How to Do It:

- Focus on key themes: Are you driven by perseverance, self-discovery, or a passion for social change? Make these themes central to your story, reflecting them in your branding, interviews, and social media content.

- Connect your story to your music: How do your life experiences influence your songwriting? Share stories that reflect the emotions or ideas in your music. For example, if your music speaks about overcoming hardship, talk about the personal struggles that inspired those songs.

3. Use Visual Storytelling

IN TODAY'S DIGITAL world, visuals are an important part of telling your story. Whether it's through album covers, music videos, social media content, or even live performances, visuals add another layer of depth to your narrative.

How to Do It:

- Create visual content that reflects your story: Think of ways to visually represent your personal journey. Album art, behind-the-scenes videos, or even stylized photoshoots that capture different moments of your career can tell a powerful story.

- Leverage social media: Use platforms like Instagram, TikTok, and YouTube to share snippets of your life—whether it's how you write songs, personal reflections, or snapshots from your daily routine. These moments help fans feel like they're part of your journey.

- Be consistent in your branding: Use a consistent visual style across your platforms to reinforce your story. Whether you're going for a minimalist aesthetic or something bold and expressive, make sure it aligns with your authentic narrative.

4. Engage with Your Audience Through Your Story

STORYTELLING IS NOT a one-way street; it's about building a relationship with your audience. Engaging with your fans by sharing your personal story creates loyalty and fosters deeper connections. People want to support artists they feel they know and understand.

How to Do It:

- Share updates and milestones: Keep your audience in the loop as you reach new goals, whether it's recording new music, booking a big gig, or hitting a personal milestone. Fans love being part of your journey.

- Ask for fan input: Engaging your audience with questions or inviting them to share their own stories helps create a deeper bond. Whether it's asking for feedback on new music or sharing fan stories that relate to your music, this interaction strengthens connections.

- Show gratitude: Make it clear that your fans are an essential part of your story. Acknowledging their support, whether through social media shoutouts or personal messages, can go a long way in building a loyal fanbase.

5. Show the Growth in Your Journey

ONE OF THE MOST POWERFUL elements of any story is growth. People are naturally drawn to stories of personal development, and your audience will be interested in seeing how you evolve as an artist and a person over time.

How to Do It:

- Document your growth: Whether it's experimenting with new sounds, collaborating with other artists, or taking on bigger projects, share the growth that you're experiencing. This gives your fans insight into your creative process and shows that you're constantly evolving.

- Reflect on your journey: Share how you've grown since starting your music career. Talk about the lessons you've learned, the struggles you've overcome, and how those experiences have shaped you as an artist.

- Be transparent about your future goals: Sharing your ambitions for the future keeps your audience invested in your journey and gives them something to root for.

Final Thoughts

EFFECTIVELY MARKETING yourself as a musician isn't just about promoting your music; it's about sharing your authentic story with the world. When you open up about your journey, struggles, and growth, you invite listeners to connect with you on a deeper level. By embracing vulnerability, identifying key themes, using visual storytelling, engaging with your audience, and showing growth, you can craft a compelling narrative that will resonate with fans and set you apart in the music industry.

Your story is unique, and it's one of the most powerful tools you have for building a lasting career in music.

Boost Your Social Media Presence with Smart Hashtags: Effective Hashtag Strategies

In the vast world of social media, hashtags are one of the most powerful tools at your disposal. They can amplify your reach, connect you with new audiences, and enhance your online presence. However, using hashtags effectively requires more than just slapping a few popular tags onto your posts. To truly boost your social media reach, you need a strategic approach. Here's how to master hashtag usage and make it work for you.

1. Understand the Purpose of Hashtags

Hashtags categorize content, making it easier for users to find posts related to specific topics. They serve as a discovery tool, allowing your content to reach beyond your immediate followers. When used correctly, hashtags can increase the visibility of your posts, attract new followers, and even help you join larger conversations within your niche.

2. Research Relevant Hashtags

Before you start using hashtags, it's essential to do some research. Identify hashtags that are relevant to your content, genre, and audience. Look at what similar artists or influencers in your niche are using. Tools like Hashtagify, RiteTag, and Instagram's own search function can help you discover popular and trending hashtags that align with your posts.

3. Mix Popular and Niche Hashtags

While it's tempting to use only popular hashtags with millions of posts, these can be highly competitive. Your content may get lost in the noise. Instead, mix popular hashtags with more niche ones that cater to a specific audience. Niche hashtags may have fewer posts, but they often attract more engaged users who are genuinely interested in the content.

For example, if you're a folk musician, you might use a combination of broad hashtags like #music[1] and #newmusic[2] along with niche ones like #folkmusic[3] and #acousticsessions[4].

4. Use Branded Hashtags

Creating a unique branded hashtag is a great way to promote your content and encourage fan engagement. A branded hashtag could be your band's name, a specific project, or even a recurring theme in your posts. Encourage your fans to use this hashtag when sharing their experiences with your music, helping to build a community around your brand.

For instance, if your band is called "The Soundwaves," you might use #SoundwavesMusic[5] as a branded hashtag, encouraging fans to tag their posts related to your music.

5. Don't Overdo It

While Instagram allows up to 30 hashtags per post, more isn't always better. Overloading your post with too many hashtags can make it look spammy and may even reduce engagement. A good rule of thumb is to use around 5 to 10 well-chosen hashtags per post. Focus on quality over quantity, ensuring that each hashtag is relevant to your content and audience.

6. Stay Updated on Trending Hashtags

Social media trends change rapidly, and staying updated on trending hashtags can help you join the conversation when it's most relevant. Whether it's a global event, a viral challenge, or a popular meme, jumping on trending hashtags can boost your visibility. However, make sure the trend aligns with your brand and content to avoid coming off as inauthentic.

---

1. https://www.interestingmusic.us/blog/hashtags/music
2. https://www.interestingmusic.us/blog/hashtags/newmusic
3. https://www.interestingmusic.us/blog/hashtags/folkmusic
4. https://www.interestingmusic.us/blog/hashtags/acousticsessions
5. https://www.interestingmusic.us/blog/hashtags/SoundwavesMusic

7. Utilize Hashtags Across Platforms

Different social media platforms have different hashtag cultures. For example, while Instagram and Twitter heavily rely on hashtags, Facebook and LinkedIn use them more sparingly. Tailor your hashtag strategy to each platform's audience and norms. On Instagram, you might use a larger number of hashtags, while on Twitter, you might focus on 1-2 targeted hashtags per tweet.

8. Analyze Hashtag Performance

To refine your hashtag strategy, regularly analyze how your hashtags are performing. Most social media platforms offer analytics tools that show which hashtags are driving engagement. Pay attention to which hashtags consistently bring in likes, comments, and new followers, and adjust your strategy accordingly.

9. Experiment and Iterate

Hashtag strategies aren't one-size-fits-all, and what works today might not work tomorrow. Don't be afraid to experiment with different combinations of hashtags, trying out new ones and retiring those that no longer serve you. The key is to keep testing and iterating your strategy based on what drives the best results.

10. Engage with Hashtag Communities

Hashtags are not just a way to categorize your content; they're also a gateway to communities. Engage with users who follow and post under the same hashtags. Like, comment, and share their content when appropriate. This kind of interaction can help you build relationships with potential fans and influencers in your niche, expanding your reach even further.

Conclusion

MASTERING HASHTAG USAGE is a powerful way to boost your social media reach and connect with a broader audience. By researching relevant hashtags, mixing popular and niche tags,

creating branded hashtags, and staying updated on trends, you can enhance your online presence and grow your fanbase. Remember, the key to an effective hashtag strategy is not just in using hashtags, but in using them thoughtfully and strategically. Keep experimenting, analyzing, and engaging with your hashtag communities to unlock the full potential of your social media efforts.

Strategies for Getting Featured on Spotify Playlists

In the digital age, getting your music noticed can be a challenge. One of the most effective ways to gain exposure is by getting your tracks featured on Spotify playlists. With millions of users worldwide, Spotify is a leading platform for music discovery. Landing a spot on a popular playlist can significantly boost your streams, followers, and overall visibility. But how do you navigate the complex world of Spotify playlists? Here are strategies to increase your chances of playlist placement.

Understanding the Spotify Playlist Ecosystem

SPOTIFY PLAYLISTS COME in various forms, each with different levels of influence:

1. Editorial Playlists: Curated by Spotify's in-house editorial team, these are the most coveted spots. Think of playlists like "New Music Friday" or "RapCaviar." Getting featured here can result in massive exposure.

2. Algorithmic Playlists: These are personalized playlists generated by Spotify's algorithms based on user listening habits. Examples include "Discover Weekly" and "Release Radar." These playlists are tailored to individual users, making them highly effective for targeting specific audiences.

3. User-Curated Playlists: These are playlists created by individual Spotify users, influencers, or brands. While they may not have the reach of editorial playlists, some user-curated lists have significant follower counts and can be an excellent way to reach niche audiences.

Strategies for Playlist Placement

1. PERFECT YOUR CRAFT
- High-Quality Production: Your music must be professionally produced. Poor sound quality will likely result in your track being skipped over by both listeners and curators.
- Strong Branding: Ensure your artist profile is polished. This includes professional cover art, a compelling bio, and consistent branding across your social media platforms. A strong brand presence signals that you're serious about your craft.

2. Optimize Your Spotify Profile
- Update Your Profile: Make sure your profile is complete with a bio, photos, and links to your social media. This helps curators understand who you are as an artist.
- Use Spotify for Artists: Claim your profile on Spotify for Artists. This gives you access to tools and analytics that are crucial for understanding your audience and improving your chances of getting featured.

3. Release Strategy
- Submit Your Music Early: Spotify allows artists to pitch their music to editorial playlists through the Spotify for Artists platform. Submitting your track at least a week before its release date increases your chances of being considered by curators.
- Consistent Releases: Regularly releasing new music keeps your profile active and gives you more opportunities to be considered for playlist placement. Aim for a steady stream of releases rather than dropping everything at once.

4. Leverage Social Media and PR
- Create Buzz: Build anticipation around your release on social media. Use platforms like Instagram, Twitter, and TikTok to engage with your audience and generate excitement. The more buzz you create, the more likely curators and listeners will take notice.

- Press Coverage: Getting press coverage can significantly boost your visibility. Send your music to blogs, online magazines, and music influencers. A positive review or feature can increase your credibility and catch the attention of playlist curators.

5. Engage with Playlist Curators

- Direct Outreach: Identify independent playlist curators in your genre and reach out to them with a polite and personalized message. Provide them with a brief introduction, a link to your track, and explain why you think it would be a good fit for their playlist.

- Networking: Attend music industry events, participate in online communities, and connect with other artists and professionals. Building relationships can lead to opportunities for playlist placements and other collaborations.

6. Leverage Data and Analytics

- Monitor Performance: Use Spotify for Artists to track how your music is performing. Pay attention to metrics like listener demographics, playlist adds, and streams. This data can help you understand what's working and refine your strategy.

- Focus on Engagement: Spotify's algorithms favor tracks with high engagement—songs that are saved, added to playlists, and listened to repeatedly. Encourage your listeners to engage with your music by sharing it, adding it to their playlists, and saving it to their libraries.

7. Collaborate with Other Artists

- Feature Collaborations: Working with other artists can help you reach new audiences. A well-timed collaboration can result in both artists being featured on each other's playlists, doubling your exposure.

- Remixes and Covers: Consider creating remixes or covers of popular songs. These can attract listeners searching for the original track and increase your chances of being included in related playlists.

8. Stay Persistent

- Patience is Key: Getting featured on a major playlist doesn't happen overnight. It requires persistence, continuous effort, and a long-term strategy. Keep creating, releasing, and promoting your music.

Conclusion

GETTING FEATURED ON Spotify playlists is a game-changer for any artist looking to expand their reach. By understanding the different types of playlists, optimizing your profile, and implementing strategic promotion, you can increase your chances of being noticed by both curators and listeners. Remember, the music industry is competitive, but with dedication and the right approach, your tracks could find their way into the ears of thousands, if not millions, of new fans.

Start implementing these strategies today, and watch your music career take off on Spotify!

Boost Your Music Video Views with YouTube Optimization

YouTube is the go-to platform for musicians and artists looking to promote their work and reach a global audience. However, with millions of videos uploaded every day, standing out can be challenging. That's where YouTube optimization comes in. By applying strategic YouTube SEO techniques, you can increase the visibility of your music videos, attract more viewers, and grow your fan base. In this guide, we'll cover essential tips and strategies to help you optimize your YouTube channel and videos for better performance.

Understanding YouTube SEO

YOUTUBE SEO REFERS to the process of optimizing your videos and channel to rank higher in YouTube's search results. Like Google, YouTube has its own algorithm that determines which videos appear at the top of search results and suggested video lists. This algorithm considers various factors, including video titles, descriptions, tags, watch time, and engagement metrics like likes, comments, and shares. By understanding how YouTube's algorithm works, you can tailor your content to meet its criteria and improve your chances of being discovered.

Optimizing Your YouTube Channel

CREATING A COMPELLING Channel Description

Your channel description is one of the first things potential viewers see when they visit your channel. It should provide a clear and engaging overview of what your channel is about. Use relevant keywords naturally throughout the description to improve your channel's visibility in search results. For example, if your channel focuses on indie music, include phrases like "indie music reviews," "up-and-coming indie artists," or "indie music videos."

Using Channel Keywords

Channel keywords help YouTube understand what your channel is about and match it with relevant searches. Choose keywords that accurately represent your niche and include them in your channel settings. Avoid keyword stuffing, which can harm your channel's performance. Instead, focus on a few well-chosen keywords that reflect the main topics you cover.

Customizing Channel Art and Logo

Professional and consistent branding is crucial for making a strong first impression. Your channel art and logo should reflect your brand identity and be visually appealing. Invest time in creating high-quality visuals that stand out. Tools like Canva or Adobe Spark can help you design custom channel art that aligns with your music's style and vibe.

Optimizing Your Music Videos

CRAFTING THE PERFECT Video Title

Your video title is one of the most critical elements for YouTube SEO. It should be catchy, descriptive, and include relevant keywords. A well-optimized title not only helps with search rankings but also encourages viewers to click on your video. For instance, instead of a generic title like "New Music Video," try something more specific like "Electrifying Indie Rock Anthem - Official Music Video."

Writing Effective Video Descriptions

The video description is an opportunity to provide more context about your video and include additional keywords. Start with a brief, engaging summary that entices viewers to watch the video. Follow this with more detailed information, such as the inspiration behind the song, lyrics, credits, and links to your social media or website. Remember to use keywords naturally and avoid keyword stuffing.

Utilizing Tags for Better Visibility

Tags are another important aspect of YouTube SEO. They help YouTube understand the content of your video and associate it with relevant searches. Use a mix of broad and specific tags that relate to your video. For example, if your video is an acoustic cover of a popular song, you might use tags like "acoustic cover," "song cover," "acoustic guitar," and the song's title and artist.

Creating Eye-Catching Thumbnails

Thumbnails are the first thing viewers see, so they play a crucial role in whether someone clicks on your video or not. A custom thumbnail that is bright, clear, and visually appealing can significantly increase your click-through rate. Use high-quality images, bold text, and contrasting colors to make your thumbnail stand out. If possible, include a close-up of a face or a recognizable element from your video.

Engaging with Your Audience

ENCOURAGING COMMENTS and Interactions

Engagement is a key factor in YouTube's algorithm, so encouraging viewers to interact with your content is essential. At the end of your videos, ask viewers to leave a comment, like, and subscribe. You can also pose a question related to the video to spark conversation. Responding to comments shows that you value your audience, which can lead to more engagement and loyalty.

Utilizing End Screens and Cards

End screens and cards are tools that allow you to promote other videos, playlists, or channels within your video. Use end screens to suggest related videos that viewers might enjoy or to prompt them to subscribe. Cards can be used throughout the video to link to other relevant content, encouraging viewers to stay on your channel longer.

Hosting Live Streams and Premieres

Live streams and premieres are great ways to engage with your audience in real-time. Live streams allow you to connect with fans directly, answer questions, and share exclusive content. Premieres give viewers the chance to watch a new video together at a scheduled time, building excitement and community around your content.

Promoting Your Videos Beyond YouTube

SHARING ON SOCIAL MEDIA

Promoting your videos on social media is essential for reaching a wider audience. Share your videos on platforms like Twitter, Instagram, Facebook, and TikTok. Use relevant hashtags, tag collaborators, and encourage your followers to share the video. Social media is also a great place to post behind-the-scenes content, teasers, and updates to keep your audience engaged.

Collaborating with Other YouTubers and Musicians

Collaborations are a powerful way to expand your reach. Partnering with other YouTubers or musicians can introduce your content to a new audience. When collaborating, choose partners whose content or style complements yours. For example, if you create electronic music, collaborating with a visual artist who specializes in music videos can enhance both of your channels.

Embedding Videos on Your Website or Blog

If you have a website or blog, embedding your YouTube videos can increase views and provide valuable content for your visitors. Include videos in relevant blog posts, or create a dedicated video page on your site. This not only helps with YouTube SEO but also keeps your website visitors engaged.

Analyzing Performance and Adjusting Strategies

USING YOUTUBE ANALYTICS

YouTube Analytics provides valuable insights into your channel's performance. Key metrics to track include watch time, audience retention, traffic sources, and demographics. Understanding these metrics can help you identify what's working and where you can improve. For example, if you notice that viewers are dropping off at a certain point in your video, you might consider editing that section or changing your content strategy.

A/B Testing Titles, Thumbnails, and Descriptions

A/B testing involves comparing two versions of a video element to see which performs better. You can A/B test titles, thumbnails, and descriptions to find out what resonates most with your audience. For example, try using two different thumbnails for the same video and track which one gets more clicks. This data-driven approach can lead to more effective YouTube optimization.

Adjusting Content Based on Audience Feedback

Listening to your audience is key to long-term success on YouTube. Pay attention to comments, likes, dislikes, and other feedback to understand what your viewers enjoy. Use this feedback to refine your content and make adjustments that align with your audience's preferences. Staying flexible and willing to adapt is crucial for growing your channel.

Conclusion

YOUTUBE IS A POWERFUL platform for musicians looking to reach a wider audience and promote their work. By optimizing your YouTube channel and videos using the SEO tips and strategies outlined in this guide, you can increase your visibility, attract more viewers, and build a loyal fan base. Remember, success on YouTube doesn't happen overnight—it requires dedication, creativity, and a willingness to learn and adapt.

FAQs

1. WHAT ARE THE BEST tools for YouTube SEO?
- Some popular tools for YouTube SEO include TubeBuddy, VidIQ, and Google Trends. These tools can help you with keyword research, video optimization, and performance analysis.

2. How often should I upload new videos to my channel?
- Consistency is key. Aim to upload new videos at least once a week, but find a schedule that works for you and stick to it. Regular uploads keep your audience engaged and improve your channel's performance in the algorithm.

3. Can I optimize older videos for better performance?
- Yes! You can update titles, descriptions, tags, and thumbnails on older videos to improve their visibility. Regularly revisiting and optimizing your older content can help drive more traffic to your channel.

4. How do I increase subscriber engagement on my channel?
- Engage with your audience by responding to comments, hosting live streams, and creating content that encourages interaction. Offering exclusive content or behind-the-scenes access to subscribers can also boost engagement.

5. Is it worth investing in YouTube ads for promoting my music videos?
- YouTube ads can be an effective way to promote your music videos, especially if you're targeting a specific audience. However, it's important to balance ad spending with organic growth strategies for the best results.

Creating Engaging Visual Content: Design Tips

In today's digital landscape, visual content is king. Whether it's a social media post, album cover, or promotional flyer, eye-catching visuals can captivate your audience and elevate your brand. However, creating engaging visual content requires more than just slapping a few images together. It's about thoughtful design, consistency, and creativity. Here are some essential design tips to help you with visual content design tips that resonate with your audience and enhance your online presence.

1. Understand Your Brand Identity

Before you start designing, it's crucial to have a clear understanding of your brand identity. What are the key messages and emotions you want to convey? What colors, fonts, and imagery best represent your brand? Establishing a consistent visual identity will make your content instantly recognizable and reinforce your brand's message.

For instance, if your music has a laid-back, beachy vibe, you might use soft blues, sandy tones, and relaxed typography in your visuals.

2. Keep It Simple

One of the most common design mistakes is overcomplicating visuals with too many elements. Simplicity is key to creating content that's easy to digest and visually appealing. Focus on a single, strong visual message, and avoid cluttering your design with unnecessary text, images, or graphics. Clean, minimalistic designs often have the most impact and are easier for your audience to engage with.

3. Use High-Quality Images

The quality of your images can make or break your visual content. Always use high-resolution images to ensure your designs look professional and polished. Blurry or pixelated images can detract from your message and make your content appear unprofessional. If you're taking your own photos, pay attention to lighting, composition, and focus to capture the best shots.

4. Leverage Color Psychology

Colors have a powerful impact on emotions and can significantly influence how your audience perceives your content. Understanding color psychology can help you choose the right color palette to evoke the desired response. For example, red is often associated with energy and passion, while blue can convey calmness and trust. Use color strategically to enhance the mood and message of your visual content.

5. Prioritize Readability

If your visual content includes text, readability should be a top priority. Choose fonts that are easy to read and avoid overly decorative or complex typefaces. Ensure there's enough contrast between your text and background so that the words stand out clearly. Additionally, limit the number of fonts you use in a single design to maintain a cohesive and professional look.

Pro Tip: Stick to one or two fonts that complement each other—one for headlines and another for body text.

6. Use the Rule of Thirds

The rule of thirds is a fundamental design principle that can help you create balanced and visually appealing compositions. Imagine your design divided into a 3x3 grid. Place key elements along these grid lines or at their intersections to create a more dynamic and engaging layout. This technique is particularly useful for photography and social media posts.

7. Incorporate White Space

White space, or negative space, is the empty area around your design elements. While it might be tempting to fill every inch of your design, white space is crucial for creating a clean and uncluttered look. It helps direct the viewer's attention to the most important parts of your design and prevents your content from feeling overwhelming.

8. Be Consistent Across Platforms

Consistency is key to building a strong visual brand. Ensure that your visual content is consistent across all platforms, from social media and your website to promotional materials. This means using the same color schemes, fonts, and design elements to create a cohesive look and feel. Consistency helps reinforce your brand identity and makes your content more recognizable to your audience.

9. Tell a Story with Your Visuals

Great visuals do more than just look good—they tell a story. Whether it's a behind-the-scenes glimpse of your creative process, a visual representation of your lyrics, or a photo that captures the essence of your music, your visuals should convey a narrative that resonates with your audience. Think about the story you want to tell with each piece of visual content and design with that narrative in mind.

10. Test and Iterate

Design is an iterative process. Don't be afraid to test different visual styles and layouts to see what resonates best with your audience. Pay attention to the engagement metrics on your posts—likes, shares, comments, and clicks can all provide valuable insights into what works and what doesn't. Use this feedback to refine your designs and continually improve your visual content strategy.

Conclusion

CREATING ENGAGING VISUAL content is a powerful way to connect with your audience and strengthen your brand. By understanding your brand identity, keeping your designs simple, leveraging color psychology, and prioritizing readability, you can craft visuals that not only look great but also resonate with your fans. Remember, consistency, storytelling, and iteration are key to mastering the art of visual content. With these design tips in mind, you'll be well on your way to creating visuals that captivate and inspire.

Tips for Starting and Sustaining Your Music Blog

In today's digital landscape, music blogging has become an influential platform for sharing insights, discovering new artists, and connecting with a global audience of music lovers. Whether you're a passionate music enthusiast, an aspiring journalist, or someone looking to break into the music industry, starting a music blog can be a fulfilling and rewarding endeavor. This guide will walk you through the basics of starting and sustaining your music blog, offering tips and strategies to help you succeed in this exciting field.

Why Start a Music Blog?

STARTING A MUSIC BLOG allows you to share your passion for music with the world. It's an opportunity to express your opinions, review albums, interview artists, and offer your unique perspective on the industry. Beyond personal satisfaction, a music blog can help you build a community of like-minded individuals, create opportunities for networking and collaboration, and even open doors to a career in music journalism or PR.

Choosing Your Niche

ONE OF THE FIRST STEPS in starting a music blog is deciding on a niche. The music industry is vast, so narrowing your focus can help you stand out. Some popular niches include:
   - Genre-specific blogs: Focus on a particular genre like hip-hop, rock, jazz, or electronic music.

- Local music scenes: Covering bands, events, and artists in a specific city or region.

- Album reviews: Writing in-depth reviews of new and classic albums.

- Music industry news: Reporting on trends, new releases, and industry changes.

- Interviews and features: Conducting interviews with artists, producers, and other industry professionals.

Choose a niche that aligns with your interests and expertise. This will make your blogging experience more enjoyable and help you connect with your target audience.

Setting Up Your Music Blog

CHOOSING A BLOGGING Platform

When setting up your blog, the first decision you'll need to make is which platform to use. There are many options available, each with its own pros and cons:

- WordPress: The most popular platform, offering flexibility and a wide range of themes and plugins.

- Blogger: A free, easy-to-use platform owned by Google, suitable for beginners.

- Wix: A user-friendly, drag-and-drop website builder with customizable templates.

Free platforms like Blogger and WordPress.com are great for beginners, but if you're serious about blogging, consider investing in a self-hosted WordPress site (WordPress.org) for greater control and customization.

Picking a Domain Name

Your domain name is your blog's address on the internet, so it's important to choose something memorable and relevant. Ideally, your domain name should be short, easy to spell, and reflective of your blog's niche. For example, if your blog focuses on indie rock, you might choose something like "IndieRockReviews.com."

Setting Up Hosting

Hosting is where your blog's files are stored, making it accessible on the internet. Reliable hosting is crucial for ensuring your blog is fast and always online. Some recommended hosting providers include:

- Bluehost: Affordable and beginner-friendly, with one-click WordPress installation.
- SiteGround: Known for excellent customer support and fast loading speeds.
- HostGator: Offers a range of plans suitable for new bloggers.

Designing Your Blog

The design of your blog plays a significant role in attracting and retaining readers. Choose a clean, responsive theme that looks good on both desktop and mobile devices. Customize your blog's appearance to reflect your personal style and the vibe of your music niche. Make sure your blog is easy to navigate, with clearly labeled categories and a search function to help visitors find content.

Creating Content for Your Music Blog

TYPES OF CONTENT

Content is the heart of your blog. To keep your readers engaged, it's important to offer a variety of content types. Some popular options include:

- Album reviews: Share your thoughts on the latest releases, classic albums, or underrated gems.
- Artist interviews: Feature interviews with musicians, producers, and other industry insiders.
- News and industry updates: Keep your readers informed about what's happening in the music world.

- Opinion pieces: Offer your perspective on trends, controversies, or changes in the industry.

Writing Engaging Posts

Writing engaging content is key to growing your blog. Focus on creating original, well-researched posts that reflect your voice and passion for music. Use a conversational tone to connect with your readers and make your blog feel personal and approachable.

Content Calendar and Consistency

Consistency is crucial for maintaining your blog's momentum. Create a content calendar to plan your posts in advance and ensure you're publishing regularly. This will help you stay organized and keep your audience engaged.

Promoting Your Music Blog

Utilizing Social Media

Social media is a powerful tool for promoting your music blog and reaching a wider audience. Platforms like Twitter, Instagram, and Facebook are great for sharing your content, engaging with readers, and connecting with other music lovers. Use hashtags, tag relevant artists and industry professionals, and participate in music-related conversations to increase your visibility.

SEO for Music Blogs

Search engine optimization (SEO) is the practice of optimizing your blog so it ranks higher in search engine results. This can drive more organic traffic to your site. Basic SEO practices include:

- Keyword research: Use tools like Google Keyword Planner to find relevant keywords for your niche.

- On-page SEO: Include keywords in your titles, headings, and throughout your posts.

- Meta descriptions: Write compelling meta descriptions that summarize your content and include keywords.

- Backlinks: Build backlinks by collaborating with other bloggers or getting featured on popular music sites.

Collaborations and Guest Posts

Collaborating with other bloggers or musicians can help you reach new audiences and grow your blog. Consider guest posting on other music blogs or inviting guest bloggers to write for your site. These collaborations can introduce your blog to a wider audience and help you build valuable relationships in the music community.

Monetizing Your Music Blog

Affiliate Marketing

Affiliate marketing involves promoting products or
services on your blog and earning a commission on any sales made through your affiliate links. For music blogs, this could include promoting music gear, concert tickets, or music streaming services. Choose affiliate programs that align with your niche and offer products your audience is likely to be interested in.

Sponsored Content

As your blog grows, you may attract offers from brands or artists looking to sponsor posts on your blog. Sponsored content can be a lucrative way to monetize your blog, but it's important to be selective and only promote products or artists that align with your values and niche.

Selling Merchandise

If you have a loyal audience, consider creating and selling branded merchandise, such as t-shirts, stickers, or posters. You can set up an online store using platforms like Shopify or integrate a store directly into your blog.

Maintaining Your Music Blog

Staying Inspired

Maintaining a blog requires dedication and creativity. To stay inspired, immerse yourself in the music scene, attend concerts, and keep discovering new artists. Surround yourself with other music enthusiasts who can inspire and motivate you.

Engaging with Your Audience

Building a community around your blog is essential for its success. Engage with your readers by responding to comments, asking for feedback, and hosting interactive features like polls or Q&A sessions. The more you interact with your audience, the more loyal they'll become.

Analyzing Blog Performance

Regularly analyzing your blog's performance can help you understand what's working and what isn't. Use tools like Google Analytics to track your blog's traffic, popular posts, and audience demographics. Use this data to refine your content strategy and improve your blog's performance over time.

Conclusion

STARTING AND MAINTAINING a music blog can be a rewarding experience, allowing you to share your love for music with the world and connect with a community of like-minded individuals. By choosing a niche, creating engaging content, and promoting your blog effectively, you can build a successful music blog that resonates with readers and makes a lasting impact.

FAQs

1. HOW MUCH TIME SHOULD I dedicate to my music blog each week?

- The time you dedicate depends on your goals and schedule. However, aim to spend at least a few hours each week on writing, promoting, and engaging with your audience.

2. Can I start a music blog with no prior experience?

- Absolutely! Many successful music bloggers started with no prior experience. Focus on learning as you go, and don't be afraid to make mistakes.

3. What are the most common challenges faced by music bloggers?

- Common challenges include finding time to blog consistently, staying motivated, and growing your audience. Overcoming these challenges requires dedication, planning, and patience.

4. How do I attract more readers to my blog?

- To attract more readers, focus on creating high-quality content, optimizing your blog for SEO, and promoting your posts on social media and through collaborations.

5. Is it possible to make a full-time income from a music blog?

- While it's possible to earn a full-time income from a music blog, it often requires time, effort, and multiple income streams such as affiliate marketing, sponsored content, and merchandise sales.

Effective Networking Techniques for Introverts

Networking is an essential skill in both personal and professional settings. It can open doors to new opportunities, provide support, and help you grow in your career. However, for many people, the thought of networking is daunting, especially if you're naturally shy or introverted. The idea of approaching strangers, initiating conversations, and building connections can feel overwhelming. But networking doesn't have to be intimidating. With the right strategies, even the shyest individuals can become effective networkers. In this blog post *"Effective Networking Techniques for Introverts"*, we'll explore practical tips for overcoming shyness and building meaningful connections that can enhance your personal and professional life.

Understanding the Importance of Networking

WHY NETWORKING MATTERS

Networking is more than just meeting people—it's about building relationships that can help you achieve your goals. Whether you're looking for a new job, trying to grow your business, or seeking advice and mentorship, a strong network can provide the support and resources you need. Networking can also lead to collaborations, partnerships, and new opportunities that you might not have discovered otherwise.

The Challenges of Networking for Shy Individuals

For shy or introverted individuals, networking can be particularly challenging. The fear of rejection, the pressure to make a good impression, and the discomfort of social interactions can all contribute to anxiety. However, it's important to remember that networking is a skill that can be developed over time. With practice and the right mindset, anyone can learn to network effectively.

Strategies for Overcoming Shyness in Networking

START WITH SMALL STEPS

If the idea of attending a large networking event feels overwhelming, start small. Begin by reaching out to people you already know—colleagues, classmates, or friends of friends. Practice initiating conversations in a low-pressure environment, and gradually build your confidence.

Prepare in Advance

Preparation is key to feeling more confident in networking situations. Before attending an event, do some research on the people who will be there. Identify a few individuals you'd like to connect with, and prepare some conversation starters or questions to ask. Having a plan can help ease anxiety and make it easier to approach others.

Focus on Listening

One of the most effective ways to overcome shyness in networking is to focus on listening rather than talking. People appreciate being heard, and active listening can help you build rapport and establish trust. Ask open-ended questions, show genuine interest in the other person's experiences, and let the conversation flow naturally.

Use Your Strengths

Shy individuals often excel at one-on-one interactions and deep conversations. Use these strengths to your advantage by seeking out smaller, more intimate networking opportunities. Rather than trying to work a room, focus on having meaningful conversations with a few people. Quality connections are more valuable than quantity.

Set Realistic Goals

Setting realistic goals can help reduce the pressure you feel when networking. Instead of aiming to meet as many people as possible, set a goal to have two or three meaningful conversations. This approach allows you to focus on building genuine connections without feeling overwhelmed.

Practice Makes Perfect

Like any skill, networking improves with practice. The more you put yourself in networking situations, the more comfortable you'll become. Start by attending smaller events, and gradually work your way up to larger gatherings. Over time, you'll build confidence and develop your own networking style.

Building and Maintaining Connections

FOLLOW UP AFTER EVENTS

Networking doesn't end when the event is over. Following up with the people you've met is crucial to building lasting connections. Send a personalized email or LinkedIn message to express your appreciation for the conversation and suggest ways to stay in touch. This simple gesture can go a long way in strengthening your network.

Offer Help and Value

Effective networking is a two-way street. Don't just focus on what others can do for you—think about how you can help them. Whether it's sharing a useful resource, offering advice, or making an introduction, providing value to others will make you a more attractive networking partner and build goodwill in your relationships.

Stay Consistent

Consistency is key to maintaining your network. Make an effort to stay in touch with your connections regularly, whether it's through periodic check-ins, sharing relevant articles, or meeting up for coffee. Staying on people's radar ensures that your relationships remain strong and mutually beneficial.

Leverage Social Media

Social media platforms like LinkedIn, Twitter, and Instagram can be powerful tools for networking. Use these platforms to connect with professionals in your industry, join relevant groups, and participate in discussions. Social media allows you to engage with others in a more relaxed, less intimidating environment, making it an excellent option for shy networkers.

Attend Industry Events and Conferences

Attending industry events and conferences is a great way to meet people with similar interests and goals. These gatherings provide a structured environment where networking is expected, making it easier to start conversations. Plus, industry events often feature workshops and panels that can give you something to talk about with other attendees.

Overcoming Common Networking Fears

FEAR OF REJECTION

The fear of rejection is one of the biggest obstacles to effective networking. It's natural to worry about being ignored or dismissed, but it's important to remember that rejection is not a reflection of your worth. If someone isn't interested in connecting, don't take it personally—simply move on to the next opportunity.

Imposter Syndrome

Imposter syndrome—the feeling that you don't belong or aren't good enough—can hold you back from networking. Remember that everyone has something valuable to offer, including you. Focus on your strengths, and remind yourself that you deserve to be there just as much as anyone else.

Social Anxiety

Social anxiety can make networking feel like an insurmountable challenge. However, there are strategies you can use to manage anxiety, such as deep breathing exercises, visualization techniques, and positive self-talk. Additionally, consider seeking support from a therapist or counselor who specializes in anxiety management.

Conclusion

NETWORKING IS A VALUABLE skill that can open doors to new opportunities, provide support, and help you achieve your goals. While it can be challenging for shy or introverted individuals, it's entirely possible to become an effective networker with the right strategies. By starting small, preparing in advance, focusing on listening, and leveraging your strengths, you can overcome shyness and build meaningful connections. Remember that networking is about quality, not quantity, and that offering value to others is key to building lasting relationships. With practice and perseverance, you'll find that networking becomes not only manageable but enjoyable.

FAQs

FAQ 1: HOW CAN I START networking if I'm shy?

Start small by reaching out to people you already know and gradually build your confidence. Preparation, listening, and setting realistic goals can also help you overcome shyness in networking situations.

FAQ 2: What should I say when networking?

Focus on asking open-ended questions and showing genuine interest in the other person. Prepare some conversation starters in advance to help ease anxiety and keep the conversation flowing.

FAQ 3: How can I follow up after a networking event?

Send a personalized email or LinkedIn message to express your appreciation for the conversation and suggest ways to stay in touch. This simple gesture can help strengthen your connection.

FAQ 4: What if I'm afraid of rejection when networking?

Remember that rejection is not a reflection of your worth. If someone isn't interested in connecting, don't take it personally—simply move on to the next opportunity.

FAQ 5: How can I use social media for networking?

Use platforms like LinkedIn, Twitter, and Instagram to connect with professionals in your industry, join relevant groups, and participate in discussions. Social media allows you to engage with others in a more relaxed, less intimidating environment.

Developing Your Music Brand: A Step-by-Step Guide

In today's dynamic music industry, where artists are not just musicians but also brands, building and maintaining a strong brand identity is crucial. Whether you're an emerging artist or an established name, your brand sets you apart, tells your story, and connects you with your audience on a deeper level. However, navigating the complexities of music branding can be challenging, particularly when it comes to solving identity and consistency issues. This blog post explores these challenges and offers strategies to help you develop a strong and cohesive music brand.

Understanding Music Branding

MUSIC BRANDING IS THE process of crafting and communicating an artist's identity, values, and message through various elements such as visuals, sound, and public persona. A well-defined brand helps artists establish a unique presence in the market, making them recognizable and memorable to fans and industry professionals alike.

Your brand is more than just your music; it's the overall experience you offer. It includes your visual style, social media presence, public image, and even the way you interact with your audience. To develop a strong brand, you must first understand who you are as an artist and what you want to convey.

Identity Challenges in Music Branding

ONE OF THE FIRST CHALLENGES artists face is defining their brand identity. This process involves deep self-reflection and understanding of your unique qualities, influences, and the message you want to share with the world.

1. Defining Your Core Message:

Your core message is the foundation of your brand. It's what you stand for and what you want your audience to take away from your music. This message should be authentic and resonate with your personal experiences and beliefs. However, articulating this message can be difficult, especially when trying to balance artistic expression with market demands.

2. Navigating Genre Expectations:

Many artists struggle with the tension between staying true to their artistic identity and meeting the expectations of their genre or target audience. It's important to find a balance where you can express your individuality while still fitting into a recognizable genre framework.

3. Evolving Without Losing Identity:

As artists grow and evolve, their brand must adapt. However, maintaining a consistent identity throughout these changes is challenging. Your brand should be flexible enough to accommodate growth, yet stable enough to retain the core elements that define you.

Consistency Challenges in Music Branding

ONCE YOU'VE ESTABLISHED your brand identity, the next challenge is maintaining consistency across all platforms and interactions. Consistency helps reinforce your brand in the minds of your audience, making it easier for them to recognize and connect with you.

1. Visual and Aesthetic Consistency:

Your visual identity, including logos, album artwork, stage design, and merchandise, should be cohesive. Every visual element should reflect your brand's core message and aesthetic. Inconsistencies in visuals can confuse your audience and dilute your brand's impact.

2. Consistent Messaging Across Platforms:

Whether it's on social media, in interviews, or during live performances, your messaging should be consistent. This includes your tone of voice, the themes you discuss, and how you interact with fans. Inconsistent messaging can lead to a disconnect between you and your audience.

3. Managing Multiple Channels:

In today's digital age, artists are expected to maintain a presence across various platforms such as Instagram, Twitter, YouTube, and streaming services. Ensuring consistency across these channels can be challenging, especially when each platform has its unique requirements and audience.

Strategies for Developing a Strong Music Brand

TO OVERCOME IDENTITY and consistency challenges, artists can implement several strategies to build a strong and lasting brand.

1. Clarify Your Vision:

Take the time to define your vision and core message. What do you want to be known for? What impact do you want your music to have? Your vision should be the guiding principle for all your branding decisions.

2. Create a Brand Style Guide:

Develop a comprehensive style guide that outlines your visual and verbal identity. This guide should include color schemes, fonts, logo usage, and guidelines for tone and messaging. A style guide ensures consistency across all platforms and materials.

3. Be Authentic:

Authenticity is key to connecting with your audience. Be true to yourself and your experiences. Your audience can sense when you're being genuine, and this builds trust and loyalty.

4. Adapt While Staying True to Your Core:

As you evolve, allow your brand to adapt, but always stay true to your core identity. For example, if your music style changes, ensure that the change aligns with your overall brand message and doesn't alienate your existing audience.

5. Engage with Your Audience:

Building a strong brand is not just about broadcasting your message; it's also about listening to and engaging with your audience. Understand their needs and preferences, and find ways to connect with them on a personal level.

Conclusion

MUSIC BRANDING IS A powerful tool that can elevate your career and set you apart in a crowded industry. By overcoming identity and consistency challenges, you can develop a strong, authentic, and cohesive brand that resonates with your audience and withstands the test of time. Remember, your brand is an extension of who you are as an artist—make it as unique and compelling as your music.

Designing and Selling Merch That Sells

In today's music industry, selling merchandise is more than just a way to make extra money; it's a powerful tool for connecting with your fans and enhancing your brand. Music merchandise can create lasting memories, provide fans with tangible pieces of their favorite artists, and offer an additional revenue stream that supports your musical endeavors. But with so much merch out there, how do you design and sell products that truly resonate with your audience? This guide will walk you through the key strategies for creating and selling music merch that sells.

Understanding Your Audience

BEFORE DIVING INTO design and production, it's crucial to understand who you're creating merch for. Knowing your audience is the foundation of a successful merch line.

Identifying Your Fan Base

Start by identifying the demographics of your fan base. Are they primarily young adults, teens, or older music enthusiasts? Do they prefer casual wear or something more unique? Understanding the preferences, lifestyle, and values of your audience will help you design products that they'll be excited to purchase. Analyzing data from social media, streaming platforms, and concert attendance can provide valuable insights into your fan base.

Surveying Fans for Ideas

One of the best ways to ensure your merch will sell is to ask your fans directly what they want. Use social media polls, email newsletters, or even in-person surveys at shows to gather feedback on potential merch ideas. Fans are often eager to share their opinions, and involving them in the process can increase their sense of connection to your brand.

Designing Merchandise That Sells

ONCE YOU HAVE A CLEAR understanding of your audience, it's time to start designing. Your merch should not only represent your music and brand but also appeal to the tastes and preferences of your fans.

Creating Unique and Memorable Designs

Originality is key when it comes to merch design. Fans are more likely to purchase items that feel unique and exclusive to your brand. Consider collaborating with graphic designers or artists who understand your aesthetic and can help bring your ideas to life. If you prefer a more hands-on approach, there are many design tools available that allow you to create your own designs. Remember, the goal is to create something that fans will be proud to wear or display.

Incorporating Band Logos and Artwork

Your band's logo is a powerful branding tool, and incorporating it into your merch is a great way to create a sense of identity and cohesion across your products. However, don't rely solely on your logo; consider integrating other visual elements, such as album artwork, tour themes, or song lyrics. This adds depth and variety to your merch line, making each item feel special and connected to your music.

Choosing the Right Merchandise Items

When it comes to selecting merchandise items, variety is important, but so is relevance. T-shirts, hoodies, and hats are staples of any merch line, but don't be afraid to think outside the box. Depending on your audience, you might consider items like tote bags, posters, vinyl records, or even custom accessories like pins or patches. The key is to offer items that your fans will actually use and enjoy.

Merchandising Strategies for Success

DESIGNING GREAT MERCH is only half the battle; the next step is to implement strategies that will help your products sell.

Offering Limited Edition Items

Creating a sense of urgency can drive sales. Limited edition items, such as tour-specific merch or special collaborations, can entice fans to make a purchase before it's too late. Announce these items with a countdown or a limited window of availability to create excitement and anticipation.

Bundling Products for Higher Sales

Bundling is an effective strategy to increase the perceived value of your products and encourage fans to buy more. For example, you could offer a bundle that includes a t-shirt, a poster, and a digital download of your latest album at a discounted price. Bundles are also a great way to move less popular items by pairing them with best-sellers.

Pricing Your Merchandise Effectively

Pricing can make or break your merch sales. Price too high, and you might alienate potential buyers; price too low, and you might not cover your costs or devalue your brand. When setting prices, consider your production costs, the perceived value of the items, and the average price points of similar products in the market. Offering a range of price points can also help cater to different segments of your audience.

Selling Your Merchandise

WITH YOUR DESIGNS AND strategies in place, it's time to start selling. Whether online or in person, the way you present and promote your merch can significantly impact sales.

Setting Up an Online Store

An online store is a must-have for any artist looking to sell merch. Platforms like Shopify, Bandcamp, and Big Cartel offer user-friendly options for setting up and managing an online store. Ensure your store is easy to navigate, with clear product descriptions, high-quality images, and a straightforward checkout process. Consider offering different payment options and shipping methods to accommodate a wider range of customers.

Selling Merch at Live Shows

Live shows are prime opportunities to sell merch, as fans are often excited and eager to take home a souvenir. Make sure your merch table is well-organized, with items clearly displayed and easy to access. Assign a dedicated person to handle sales so you can focus on performing and interacting with fans. Offering exclusive tour merch or discounts for on-the-spot purchases can also boost sales.

Using Social Media for Merch Sales

Social media is a powerful tool for promoting your merch. Announce new products, limited editions, or sales on platforms like Instagram, Facebook, and Twitter. Use high-quality photos and engaging captions to capture attention. You can also leverage social media features like Instagram Shopping or Facebook Shops to make it easier for fans to purchase directly through your posts.

Maximizing Merchandising Profits

TO ENSURE YOUR MERCH efforts are profitable, it's important to manage costs, inventory, and production efficiently.

Managing Inventory and Costs

Keeping track of your inventory is crucial to avoid overselling or running out of popular items. Use inventory management software to monitor stock levels and sales trends. When it comes to production, aim for a balance between quality and cost. While it's tempting to go for the cheapest option, remember that low-quality merch can reflect poorly on your brand and lead to dissatisfied customers.

Expanding Your Merch Line Over Time

As your fan base grows, so should your merch line. Introduce new products gradually to keep your offerings fresh and exciting. Pay attention to what sells well and consider expanding those categories. For instance, if your t-shirts are a hit, you might experiment with different designs, colors, or styles.

Collaborating with Other Artists or Brands

Collaborations can add value and excitement to your merch line. Partnering with other artists, designers, or even brands can lead to unique and highly sought-after products. Collaborations not only expand your reach but also offer opportunities for creative cross-promotion.

Conclusion

DESIGNING AND SELLING music merchandise is both an art and a science. By understanding your audience, creating appealing designs, implementing smart merchandising strategies, and effectively selling your products, you can turn your merch into a powerful tool for fan engagement and revenue generation. Start small, stay true to your brand, and always listen to your fans. With time and effort, your merch can become a key component of your musical career.

FAQs

1. HOW DO I KNOW WHAT type of merch my fans will like?
 - Start by analyzing your fan demographics and gathering direct feedback through surveys and social media polls. Understanding their preferences will guide your design choices.

2. What are the best platforms for selling music merchandise online?

BRANDING & NETWORKING SUCCESS FOR BANDS

- Popular platforms include Shopify, Bandcamp, and Big Cartel. Each offers unique features, so choose one that best suits your needs for ease of use, customization, and integration.

3. How can I promote my merch without feeling too salesy?

- Engage your fans by sharing behind-the-scenes content, stories about the design process, and limited-time offers. Authenticity and transparency go a long way in building trust and excitement.

4. Is it better to produce merch in-house or use a third-party service?

- It depends on your resources and goals. In-house production offers control and potentially higher margins, while third-party services can handle logistics and scale more easily.

5. How do I handle shipping and fulfillment for online orders?

- Consider using fulfillment services like Printful or ShipStation to manage shipping efficiently. They can help streamline the process, allowing you to focus on creating and promoting your merch.

Fan Demographics: Analyzing Data for Targeted Marketing

Understanding your audience is the cornerstone of effective marketing. Whether you're a musician, content creator, or business owner, knowing who your fans are allows you to tailor your messaging, products, and services to meet their needs and preferences. This is where fan demographics come into play. By analyzing demographic data, you can gain valuable insights into your audience's age, gender, location, interests, and more. In this blog post, we'll explore the importance of fan demographics, discuss how to analyze this data, and provide strategies for using it to create targeted marketing campaigns that resonate with your audience.

The Importance of Understanding Fan Demographics

PERSONALIZED MARKETING

One of the biggest advantages of understanding fan demographics is the ability to create personalized marketing campaigns. When you know who your fans are, you can craft messages that speak directly to them, addressing their specific interests, needs, and pain points. This level of personalization can lead to higher engagement rates, increased loyalty, and ultimately, more conversions.

Optimized Content Creation

Content creation is at the heart of any successful marketing strategy. By analyzing fan demographics, you can determine what type of content resonates most with your audience. For example, if your fan base consists mainly of younger individuals, you might focus on creating content that's more visual and shareable on platforms like

Instagram or TikTok. On the other hand, if your audience is older, you might prioritize long-form content and educational resources.

Efficient Ad Spend

When you understand your audience, you can allocate your ad budget more effectively. Instead of casting a wide net and hoping for the best, targeted marketing allows you to focus your resources on the platforms, channels, and demographics that are most likely to convert. This not only saves you money but also increases the return on investment (ROI) for your marketing efforts.

Better Product Development

Fan demographics can also inform product development. By understanding the preferences and behaviors of your audience, you can create products and services that are more likely to meet their needs and desires. This can lead to higher customer satisfaction and more repeat business.

Key Fan Demographics to Analyze

AGE

Age is one of the most important demographics to consider. Different age groups have different preferences, behaviors, and spending habits. For example, younger fans might be more interested in social media interactions and digital products, while older fans might prefer traditional media and physical goods.

Gender

Gender can also play a significant role in shaping your marketing strategy. By understanding the gender distribution of your audience, you can create campaigns that resonate with specific groups. For instance, if your fan base is predominantly female, you might focus on themes and messaging that appeal to women.

Location

Geographical data is crucial for understanding where your fans are located. This can help you tailor your marketing efforts to specific regions, cities, or even neighborhoods. Location data can also inform decisions about where to host events, how to price products, and which markets to target next.

Interests and Hobbies

Understanding your fans' interests and hobbies allows you to create content and products that align with their passions. For example, if a large portion of your audience is interested in fitness, you might create content that ties your brand to healthy living or active lifestyles.

Income Level

Income level can influence purchasing decisions and should be considered when pricing products or creating marketing campaigns. If your audience has a higher income, they might be more interested in premium products and services. Conversely, if your audience has a lower income, you might focus on affordability and value.

Education Level

Education level can provide insights into the type of content and messaging that will resonate with your audience. For example, a more educated audience might prefer detailed, data-driven content, while a less educated audience might respond better to simple, straightforward messaging.

How to Gather and Analyze Fan Demographics

STEP 1: USE SOCIAL Media Analytics

Social media platforms like Facebook, Instagram, and Twitter offer built-in analytics tools that provide demographic data about your followers. These tools can give you insights into the age, gender, location, and interests of your audience. Regularly reviewing these analytics can help you stay informed about who your fans are and how they're engaging with your content.

Step 2: Conduct Surveys and Polls

Surveys and polls are effective ways to gather demographic data directly from your audience. You can ask questions about age, gender, location, interests, and more. Tools like Google Forms, SurveyMonkey, and social media polls make it easy to create and distribute surveys to your fans.

Step 3: Analyze Website Traffic Data

Tools like Google Analytics provide detailed information about the demographics of your website visitors. You can see data on age, gender, location, and even the devices and browsers your audience is using. This information can help you understand who's visiting your site and how they're interacting with your content.

Step 4: Monitor Purchase Data

If you're selling products or services, analyzing purchase data can give you valuable insights into your audience's demographics. Look at the age, gender, and location of your customers, as well as their purchasing habits. This can help you identify trends and tailor your offerings to better meet their needs.

Step 5: Use Third-Party Data Providers

There are many third-party data providers that can help you gather demographic information about your audience. These services often aggregate data from various sources to provide a more comprehensive view of your audience. Some popular options include Nielsen, Comscore, and Experian.

Strategies for Targeted Marketing Based on Demographics

CREATE SEGMENTED CAMPAIGNS

One of the most effective ways to use demographic data is to create segmented marketing campaigns. By dividing your audience into smaller groups based on age, gender, location, or interests, you can create more personalized and relevant messaging. For example, you might create separate email campaigns for different age groups, with each campaign highlighting products or content that's most likely to appeal to that group.

Tailor Your Content Strategy

Use demographic data to inform your content strategy. If your audience is predominantly young, focus on creating content that's visually engaging and easily shareable. If your audience is older, you might prioritize more in-depth articles, videos, and educational content. Tailoring your content to the preferences of your audience can lead to higher engagement and more meaningful connections with your fans.

Optimize Your Ad Targeting

Demographic data is invaluable when it comes to ad targeting. Platforms like Facebook and Google Ads allow you to target ads based on age, gender, location, interests, and more. By using this data to refine your ad targeting, you can ensure that your ads are being seen by the people who are most likely to engage with them.

Personalize Your Messaging

Personalization is key to effective marketing. Use demographic data to create personalized messages that speak directly to your audience's needs and interests. Whether it's through email marketing, social media, or direct mail, personalized messaging can increase engagement and build stronger relationships with your fans.

Adjust Your Pricing and Promotions

Consider the income level and purchasing habits of your audience when setting prices and creating promotions. If your audience is price-sensitive, you might offer discounts, bundles, or loyalty programs to encourage purchases. On the other hand, if your audience values premium products, you might focus on highlighting the quality and exclusivity of your offerings.

Conclusion

UNDERSTANDING FAN DEMOGRAPHICS is essential for creating targeted marketing campaigns that resonate with your audience. By analyzing data on age, gender, location, interests, and more, you can gain valuable insights into who your fans are and what they want. This knowledge allows you to personalize your marketing efforts, optimize your content strategy, and allocate your resources more effectively. Start by gathering demographic data using social media analytics, surveys, website traffic data, and purchase data. Then, use this information to create segmented campaigns, tailor your content, and refine your ad targeting. With a deep understanding of your audience, you can create marketing campaigns that truly connect with your fans and drive meaningful results.

FAQs

FAQ 1: WHAT ARE FAN demographics?
 Fan demographics refer to the statistical characteristics of your audience, such as age, gender, location, interests, income level, and education. Understanding these demographics helps you tailor your marketing efforts to better connect with your audience.
 FAQ 2: How can I gather demographic data about my audience?
 You can gather demographic data using social media analytics, surveys, website traffic tools like Google Analytics, purchase data, and third-party data providers.
 FAQ 3: Why is it important to understand fan demographics?
 Understanding fan demographics allows you to create personalized marketing campaigns, optimize content, allocate your ad budget more effectively, and develop products that meet your audience's needs.
 FAQ 4: How can I use fan demographics for targeted marketing?

Use fan demographics to create segmented campaigns, tailor your content strategy, optimize ad targeting, personalize your messaging, and adjust pricing and promotions based on your audience's preferences.

FAQ 5: What tools can help me analyze fan demographics?

Tools like Google Analytics, social media analytics platforms, SurveyMonkey, and third-party data providers like Nielsen and Comscore can help you analyze fan demographics and gain valuable insights into your audience.

Music Video Storyboarding: Solving Visual Narrative Challenges

In the world of music videos, visuals play an equally important role as the music itself. But creating compelling visuals isn't just about picking up a camera and shooting; it starts with a solid plan. That's where storyboarding comes in. Storyboarding is the art of planning out each scene, shot, and visual element of a music video, ensuring that the final product is cohesive, engaging, and in sync with the music. But storyboarding isn't without its challenges, especially when it comes to translating abstract ideas into a visual narrative. This article will dive into the importance of storyboarding in music videos and explore how to solve common visual narrative challenges.

Understanding the Basics of Storyboarding

WHAT IS A STORYBOARD?

A storyboard is a visual representation of how a music video will unfold, shot by shot. It's essentially a series of drawings that show how each scene will look, including camera angles, movements, and transitions. Think of it as a comic strip, but with a focus on planning out every detail of the music video. Each frame of the storyboard serves as a guide for the production team, helping to visualize the final product before any filming begins.

Key Elements of an Effective Storyboard

VISUALIZING SCENES

One of the main purposes of a storyboard is to visualize scenes before they are filmed. This involves breaking down the song into different parts and determining how each part will be represented visually. It's about thinking through every moment and deciding what will be seen on screen and how it will connect with the music.

Detailing Camera Angles and Movements

A well-thought-out storyboard includes specific details about camera angles and movements. Will the camera be stationary, or will it follow the subject? Will there be close-ups or wide shots? These decisions impact how the audience experiences the music video and must be carefully planned out in the storyboard.

Integrating the Music and Lyrics

The visuals in a music video need to align with the music and lyrics. This integration is a critical part of storyboarding. Whether it's a literal interpretation of the lyrics or a more abstract representation, the storyboard should reflect how the visuals will enhance the music and convey the intended message or emotion.

Identifying Common Visual Narrative Challenges

CHALLENGE 1: TRANSLATING Abstract Concepts into Visuals

Music videos often deal with abstract concepts, such as emotions, ideas, or themes that aren't easy to depict visually. Translating these abstract concepts into a visual narrative is one of the biggest challenges in storyboarding. It requires creativity, imagination, and a deep understanding of the song's message.

Challenge 2: Ensuring Cohesiveness in the Storyline

Another challenge is ensuring that the music video tells a cohesive story from start to finish. This involves maintaining a consistent tone, style, and flow throughout the video. A disjointed or confusing narrative can detract from the impact of the video, so it's crucial to map out the storyline in the storyboard.

Challenge 3: Balancing Artistic Vision with Practical Constraints

While creativity is key, practical constraints like budget and time often limit what can be achieved. Balancing artistic vision with these constraints is a common challenge in music video production.

Budgetary Limitations

A GRAND VISION MAY require expensive locations, props, or special effects that aren't feasible within the available budget. Storyboarding helps identify where compromises can be made without sacrificing the overall vision.

Time Constraints

Time is another factor that can impact the storyboarding process. Tight deadlines may mean that certain shots or scenes need to be simplified or cut altogether. Storyboarding allows for careful planning to ensure that the video can be completed on time.

Challenge 4: Capturing Audience Emotion and Attention

Finally, a major challenge in music video storyboarding is creating visuals that capture the audience's emotion and attention. The visuals should not only complement the music but also evoke the intended emotional response from the audience.

Step-by-Step Guide to Effective Music Video Storyboarding

STEP 1: ANALYZING THE Song's Lyrics and Theme

The first step in storyboarding a music video is to analyze the song's lyrics and theme. This involves understanding the message, emotion, and mood that the song conveys. Once you have a clear grasp of the song's essence, you can start brainstorming visual ideas that align with the music.

Step 2: Brainstorming Visual Ideas

After analyzing the song, the next step is brainstorming visual ideas. This is where creativity comes into play. Consider different ways to represent the song's message visually. Will you go for a literal interpretation of the lyrics, or will you use metaphors and symbolism to convey the theme?

Collaborating with the Creative Team

Brainstorming is often a collaborative process that involves input from the director, cinematographer, and other members of the creative team. Collaboration ensures that all ideas are considered and that the final storyboard reflects a unified vision.

Step 3: Sketching the Storyboard Frames

Once you have a clear idea of the visuals, it's time to start sketching the storyboard frames. Each frame should represent a specific moment in the music video, including details about the camera angle, movement, and transition.

Using Storyboarding Software vs. Hand-drawn Sketches

There are different ways to create a storyboard, from traditional hand-drawn sketches to digital storyboarding software. Both methods have their advantages. Hand-drawn sketches offer a more personal touch, while digital tools provide more precision and flexibility.

Step 4: Reviewing and Refining the Storyboard

Storyboarding is an iterative process, meaning that it often involves multiple drafts and revisions. After the initial sketches are done, it's important to review and refine the storyboard to ensure that it effectively communicates the intended visual narrative.

Step 5: Finalizing the Storyboard for Production

The final step in the storyboarding process is to finalize the storyboard for production. This involves making any last-minute adjustments and ensuring that the storyboard is clear and detailed enough to guide the production team during filming.

Tools and Techniques for Storyboarding

POPULAR STORYBOARDING Software for Music Videos

There are several software options available for creating storyboards, each with its unique features. Popular choices include Adobe Storyboard, Storyboarder, and Toon Boom Storyboard Pro. These tools offer a range of functionalities, from basic sketching to advanced animation and collaboration features.

Traditional Storyboarding Techniques

Pencil and Paper

For those who prefer a more traditional approach, pencil and paper are still a popular choice for storyboarding. This method allows for quick sketches and is often favored by those with strong drawing skills.

Digital Tools

Digital tools, on the other hand, offer greater flexibility and the ability to make changes easily. Many digital storyboarding programs also come with pre-made templates and assets, making it easier to create detailed and professional-looking storyboards.

Conclusion

RECAP OF STORYBOARDING Importance in Music Videos

Storyboarding is a vital part of the music video production process. It serves as a blueprint that guides the entire production, ensuring that the final product is visually engaging, cohesive, and in sync with the music.

Final Thoughts on Overcoming Visual Narrative Challenges

While storyboarding comes with its challenges, from translating abstract concepts into visuals to balancing artistic vision with practical constraints, it is an essential tool for overcoming these obstacles. With careful planning and creativity, you can create a music video that not only tells a compelling story but also resonates with your audience.

FAQs

FAQ 1: WHAT IS THE most challenging part of music video storyboarding?

The most challenging part is often translating abstract concepts and emotions into visual elements that are both engaging and understandable.

FAQ 2: How long does it take to storyboard a music video?

The time it takes can vary depending on the complexity of the video, but it typically ranges from a few days to several weeks.

FAQ 3: Can I create a storyboard without professional software?

Yes, you can create a storyboard using traditional methods like pencil and paper, or you can use free digital tools if professional software is not accessible.

FAQ 4: How detailed should a music video storyboard be?

A storyboard should be detailed enough to guide the production team through each shot and scene, but it doesn't need to be overly complex.

FAQ 5: What are the key skills needed for effective storyboarding?

Key skills include creativity, attention to detail, an understanding of visual storytelling, and the ability to translate ideas into visual form.

Effective Press Releases: Crafting Newsworthy Announcements

In the digital age, where news travels faster than ever, an effective press release remains a powerful tool for getting your message out to the masses. Whether you're announcing a new product, a major event, or a significant achievement, crafting a newsworthy press release can make the difference between being noticed or ignored. But what makes a press release effective? How do you ensure your announcement stands out in a crowded media landscape? In this blog post, we'll explore the essential components of a compelling press release, provide tips for making your announcement newsworthy, and share strategies for maximizing its impact.

The Importance of a Well-Crafted Press Release

BUILDING BRAND AWARENESS

A well-crafted press release is an excellent way to build brand awareness. By distributing your news to media outlets, you can reach a broader audience and establish your brand as a credible and authoritative source in your industry. This can lead to increased visibility, greater trust, and more opportunities for growth.

Driving Traffic and Engagement

Press releases are not just about getting media coverage—they can also drive traffic to your website, boost social media engagement, and generate leads. When your announcement resonates with your audience, they're more likely to visit your site, share your news, and engage with your brand.

Enhancing SEO

Press releases can also enhance your search engine optimization (SEO) efforts. By incorporating relevant keywords and backlinks, your press release can improve your site's search engine rankings and increase its visibility online. This can lead to more organic traffic and higher conversion rates.

Key Components of an Effective Press Release

COMPELLING HEADLINE

The headline is the first thing readers will see, so it's crucial to make it compelling. A strong headline grabs attention, conveys the main point of your announcement, and entices the reader to learn more. Keep it concise, clear, and impactful—aim for no more than 10-12 words.

Engaging Lead Paragraph

The lead paragraph is where you capture your reader's interest and provide the essential details of your announcement. This section should answer the "who," "what," "when," "where," and "why" of your news. It's important to be concise yet informative, giving readers a reason to continue reading.

Informative Body

The body of your press release should provide additional context and details about your announcement. This is where you elaborate on the significance of your news, provide supporting facts, and include quotes from key stakeholders. Use clear and concise language, and make sure each paragraph adds value to the reader.

Quotes from Key Stakeholders

Including quotes from key stakeholders—such as company executives, industry experts, or customers—can add credibility and a personal touch to your press release. These quotes should highlight the importance of your announcement and provide insights or perspectives that enhance the story.

Call to Action (CTA)

Your press release should include a clear call to action, guiding readers on what to do next. Whether it's visiting your website, signing up for an event, or contacting you for more information, a strong CTA can help drive engagement and conversions.

Contact Information

Always include contact information at the end of your press release. This should include the name, phone number, and email address of a person who can provide more details or arrange interviews. Make it easy for journalists and interested parties to reach out to you.

Tips for Crafting Newsworthy Announcements

FOCUS ON WHAT'S TRULY Newsworthy

Not every announcement is newsworthy, so it's important to focus on what makes your news stand out. Ask yourself: Does this announcement offer something new or unique? Is it relevant to a broader audience? Will it have a significant impact on the industry or community? Highlighting these aspects can make your press release more compelling to journalists and readers alike.

Keep It Concise and Clear

Journalists and readers are busy, so keep your press release concise and to the point. Aim for 400-600 words, and avoid jargon or overly technical language. The goal is to convey your message clearly and efficiently, making it easy for anyone to understand.

Use Data and Statistics

Including data and statistics can add credibility to your press release and make your announcement more persuasive. Whether it's sales figures, market trends, or customer satisfaction ratings, concrete numbers can help support your claims and make your news more impactful.

Leverage Multimedia

Incorporating multimedia elements like images, videos, or infographics can make your press release more engaging and shareable. Visual content can help illustrate your story, grab attention, and make your announcement more memorable.

Tailor Your Press Release for Different Audiences

Different audiences may be interested in different aspects of your announcement, so consider tailoring your press release to meet their needs. For example, you might create different versions of your release for industry insiders, local media, and consumers, each highlighting the most relevant points for that audience.

Maximizing the Impact of Your Press Release

DISTRIBUTE TO THE RIGHT Channels

To maximize the impact of your press release, it's important to distribute it to the right channels. This includes both traditional media outlets (such as newspapers, magazines, and TV stations) and digital platforms (such as online news sites, blogs, and social media). Consider using a press release distribution service to reach a wider audience.

Leverage Social Media

Social media can be a powerful tool for amplifying your press release. Share your announcement on your social media channels, and encourage your followers to do the same. Use relevant hashtags to increase visibility and reach a broader audience.

Follow Up with Journalists

Don't just send out your press release and hope for the best—follow up with journalists who might be interested in your story. A personalized email or phone call can help ensure your press release gets noticed and increases the chances of media coverage.

Track and Analyze Results

After your press release has been distributed, track its performance using tools like Google Analytics, social media insights, and press coverage reports. Analyzing the results can help you understand what worked well and what could be improved for future releases.

Conclusion

CRAFTING AN EFFECTIVE press release requires careful planning, clear communication, and a focus on what's truly newsworthy. By following the tips outlined in this blog post, you can create press releases that not only capture the attention of journalists and readers but also drive engagement and build your brand's reputation. Remember to keep your announcements concise, use compelling data, and leverage multimedia to make your news stand out. With the right strategy, your press releases can become powerful tools for spreading your message and achieving your goals.

FAQs

FAQ 1: WHAT IS THE main purpose of a press release?

The main purpose of a press release is to communicate important news or announcements to the media and the public, with the goal of generating coverage and building brand awareness.

FAQ 2: How long should a press release be?

A press release should typically be between 400-600 words. It's important to keep it concise while still providing all the necessary details.

FAQ 3: What should be included in a press release?

A press release should include a compelling headline, an engaging lead paragraph, an informative body, quotes from key stakeholders, a call to action, and contact information.

FAQ 4: How can I make my press release more newsworthy?

To make your press release more newsworthy, focus on what makes your announcement unique, relevant, and impactful. Use data and statistics to support your claims and consider incorporating multimedia elements.

FAQ 5: What's the best way to distribute a press release?

The best way to distribute a press release is through a combination of traditional media outlets, digital platforms, and social media. Consider using a press release distribution service to reach a wider audience.

Creating Engaging Content: Storytelling for Music Blogs

In the world of music blogging, content is king. But not just any content—content that resonates, engages, and leaves a lasting impression on your readers. One of the most powerful tools at your disposal is storytelling. By weaving compelling narratives into your blog, you can connect with your audience on a deeper level, turning casual readers into loyal followers. This post will guide you through the art of storytelling in music blogs, helping you create content that not only informs but also captivates.

Understanding the Elements of a Good Story

BEFORE DIVING INTO how to incorporate storytelling into your music blog, it's essential to understand what makes a story engaging.

What Makes a Story Engaging?

At the heart of every good story are three key components: characters, conflict, and resolution. Characters give your story a face, conflict drives the narrative forward, and resolution provides closure, leaving your readers satisfied. In the context of a music blog, your "characters" could be yourself, your band, or even your fans. The "conflict" might be the challenges faced during your musical journey, while the "resolution" is how you overcame them or what you learned.

The Role of Emotion in Storytelling

Emotion is the glue that binds a story to its audience. When readers feel something—whether it's excitement, nostalgia, or empathy—they're more likely to stay engaged and remember your story. Music itself is deeply emotional, and by tapping into those emotions through your blog, you can create a powerful connection with your readers.

Creating Relatable and Authentic Narratives

Authenticity is crucial in storytelling. Readers can easily spot when a story feels forced or insincere. To create narratives that resonate, focus on being genuine. Share your real experiences, thoughts, and feelings. Authentic stories are not only more engaging but also help build trust with your audience.

Incorporating Storytelling in Music Blogs

NOW THAT YOU KNOW WHAT makes a story compelling, let's explore how to incorporate storytelling into your music blog.

Sharing Personal Journeys

One of the most impactful ways to engage your audience is by sharing your personal journey as an artist. Talk about how you got started in music, the challenges you've faced, and the milestones you've achieved. These stories not only humanize you as an artist but also allow your readers to feel a part of your journey.

For example, you could write about the inspiration behind a particular song or album, the struggles you encountered while recording, or the emotions you experienced when you first performed it live. By inviting readers into your world, you create a bond that goes beyond the music itself.

Writing About the Creative Process

Your creative process is another rich source of storytelling material. Fans are often curious about how their favorite songs come to life, and sharing this behind-the-scenes content can be incredibly engaging. Write about where you find inspiration, how you overcome creative blocks, and the evolution of a song from an idea to a finished product.

For instance, you could narrate the story of a song that took an unexpected turn during production, or how a last-minute change in lyrics completely transformed its meaning. These insights not only provide valuable content but also deepen the connection between you and your readers.

Engaging with Fan Stories

Your fans' stories are just as important as your own. Encouraging fans to share their experiences and incorporating these into your blog can create a sense of community and belonging. Whether it's a fan who traveled miles to see your concert or someone who found solace in your music during tough times, these stories add richness and diversity to your blog.

Consider featuring fan stories as guest posts or dedicating a section of your blog to fan experiences. This not only diversifies your content but also shows your appreciation for the people who support you.

Techniques for Effective Storytelling

TO MAKE YOUR STORIES as engaging as possible, it's essential to use the right techniques.

Using Vivid Imagery and Descriptive Language

Great stories paint pictures in the minds of readers. Use vivid imagery and descriptive language to bring your narratives to life. Instead of simply telling your readers what happened, show them by describing the sights, sounds, and emotions you experienced. For example, instead of saying "the concert was amazing," describe the feeling of stepping onto the stage, the roar of the crowd, and the energy that filled the air.

Structuring Your Story for Maximum Impact

A well-structured story keeps readers hooked from beginning to end. Start with a strong opening that grabs attention, build up the narrative in the middle, and conclude with a satisfying resolution. This classic structure works well because it mirrors the natural flow of human experiences.

For a music blog, this might mean starting with an intriguing anecdote or question, developing the story with personal insights or details about your music, and concluding with what you learned or how it affected your career.

Pacing and Rhythm in Your Writing

Just like a song, a story needs the right pacing and rhythm to keep it engaging. Vary the length of your sentences and paragraphs to create a natural flow. Use short, punchy sentences to convey excitement or urgency, and longer, more detailed sentences for reflection or description. The rhythm of your writing can significantly impact how your story is received.

Creating Content That Resonates

TO ENSURE YOUR STORYTELLING content resonates with your audience, it's important to align it with your brand and tailor it to your readers.

Aligning Stories with Your Brand

Your stories should reflect your musical identity and the image you want to project. Whether you're a rock band with a rebellious edge or a solo artist known for introspective lyrics, your storytelling should be consistent with your brand. This consistency helps reinforce your identity and makes your content more memorable.

Writing for Your Target Audience

Consider who your readers are and what they're interested in when crafting your stories. If your audience is primarily young, emerging artists, they might appreciate stories about the struggles of breaking into the industry. If they're long-time fans, they might be more interested in behind-the-scenes tales or deep dives into your music. Tailoring your content to your audience ensures it resonates more deeply.

Incorporating Visuals to Enhance Your Stories

Visuals are a powerful complement to written narratives. Incorporate images, videos, or graphics to enhance your stories and make them more engaging. For example, include photos from the studio session you're writing about, or share a short video clip of a live performance. Visual content not only grabs attention but also helps illustrate your story, making it more immersive.

Promoting Your Storytelling Content

ONCE YOU'VE CRAFTED your stories, it's time to share them with the world.

Sharing Stories on Social Media

Social media is an excellent platform for promoting your storytelling content. Share snippets of your blog posts, accompanied by eye-catching visuals, to entice your followers to read the full story. Use platforms like Instagram, Twitter, and Facebook to expand your reach and engage with a wider audience.

Collaborating with Other Bloggers and Artists

Collaborations can amplify your storytelling efforts. Consider teaming up with other bloggers or artists for guest posts, interviews, or collaborative storytelling projects. These collaborations can introduce your content to new audiences and provide fresh perspectives for your blog.

Encouraging Reader Interaction and Feedback

Engagement doesn't stop when you hit "publish." Encourage your readers to leave comments, share your posts, and participate in discussions. Ask open-ended questions at the end of your posts to invite feedback, and consider highlighting reader comments or stories in future content. This interaction not only builds community but also provides valuable insights into what your audience enjoys.

Conclusion

STORYTELLING IS A POWERFUL tool in the world of music blogging. By creating engaging, authentic narratives, you can connect with your audience on a deeper level, turning your blog into more than just a source of information—it becomes a space for connection, inspiration, and community. Start experimenting with storytelling in your blog, and watch as your content becomes more engaging and impactful.

FAQs

1. WHAT TYPES OF STORIES resonate best with music blog readers?
- Personal journeys, behind-the-scenes insights, and fan experiences often resonate the most, as they create a deeper connection with readers.
2. How can I improve my storytelling skills for blogging?
- Practice regularly, read other blogs for inspiration, and focus on being authentic. Experiment with different techniques and find what works best for you.
3. Should I focus on personal stories or broader industry topics?
- A mix of both can be effective. Personal stories create a strong connection, while broader topics can attract a wider audience and provide valuable insights.
4. How often should I incorporate storytelling in my blog posts?
- It's a good idea to include storytelling in most of your posts, but the extent can vary depending on the topic. Even a short anecdote can enhance a more factual piece.
5. What are some common mistakes to avoid in storytelling?

BRANDING & NETWORKING SUCCESS FOR BANDS

- Avoid being overly dramatic or inauthentic, as this can turn readers off. Also, be mindful of pacing—don't rush through the story or drag it out too long.

Best Practices for Booking Gigs Successfully

Booking gigs is an essential part of building your music career, but it can also be one of the most challenging aspects, especially when communication with venues doesn't go smoothly. Whether it's slow responses, unclear expectations, or last-minute changes, poor communication can derail your plans and cause unnecessary stress. Here's how to troubleshoot common issues and improve your gig booking processes through better venue communication.

1. Research Before Reaching Out

BEFORE CONTACTING A venue, do your homework. Understand the type of music they typically host, their audience, and the size and layout of the space. This information will help you tailor your pitch and show that you're serious about playing there. It also ensures that the venue is a good fit for your music, saving you time and potential frustration later on.

2. Craft a Clear and Concise Pitch

YOUR INITIAL OUTREACH should be professional and to the point. Introduce yourself, describe your music, and explain why you want to play at their venue. Include links to your music, social media profiles, and any relevant press or past gig experiences. Keep it brief—venue managers are busy and appreciate clear, concise communication.

Example Pitch:
"Hi [Venue Name],

I'm [Your Name], a [genre] musician from [city]. I've been following [venue's name] and believe my music would resonate with your audience. I'd love to discuss the possibility of performing at your venue. You can listen to my latest tracks [here], and see some recent live performances [here]. Let me know if you'd be interested, and we can talk details.

Looking forward to hearing from you!
Best,
[Your Name]"

3. Follow Up Respectfully

IF YOU DON'T HEAR BACK within a reasonable timeframe (usually one to two weeks), send a polite follow-up. Venue managers often receive a high volume of emails, and a respectful nudge can help your message stand out without coming off as pushy.

Example Follow-Up:
"Hi [Venue Name],

I wanted to follow up on my previous email about performing at your venue. I'm very interested in the opportunity and would love to discuss it further if you have the time. I've included the original email below for your reference.

Thanks again for considering my request!
Best,
[Your Name]"

4. Be Clear About Expectations

ONCE YOU'VE ESTABLISHED contact, it's important to be clear about expectations from both sides. Discuss details like the date and time of the gig, payment, soundcheck times, load-in/load-out procedures, and any technical requirements. Putting everything in writing helps avoid misunderstandings and ensures that both you and the venue are on the same page.

5. Be Responsive and Professional

TIMELY COMMUNICATION is key to maintaining a good relationship with venues. Respond promptly to emails and messages, and be professional in all your interactions. If you have any concerns or need clarification, don't hesitate to ask, but always do so respectfully.

6. Prepare for Last-Minute Changes

EVEN WITH THE BEST planning, last-minute changes can happen. Venues might adjust set times, or there could be unforeseen technical issues. Stay flexible and have backup plans when possible. Maintaining a calm and professional demeanor in these situations shows the venue that you're reliable and easy to work with, increasing your chances of being booked again in the future.

7. Confirm Details in Advance

A DAY OR TWO BEFORE the gig, send a confirmation email to the venue to ensure everything is set. Confirm the time, address, and any other important details. This not only shows professionalism but also helps avoid any last-minute surprises.

Example Confirmation Email:
"Hi [Venue Name],
I'm excited about the upcoming gig on [date]! I just wanted to confirm the details: [list of key details, such as set time, load-in time, and payment arrangements]. Please let me know if there are any changes or if anything else is needed from my side.
Looking forward to it!

Best,
[Your Name]"

8. Maintain Good Relationships

AFTER THE GIG, SEND a thank-you note to the venue, expressing your appreciation for the opportunity to perform. If things went well, mention your interest in playing there again. Building and maintaining good relationships with venues is crucial for securing future bookings and can lead to better opportunities down the road.

Example Thank-You Note:

"Hi [Venue Name],

Thank you so much for having me at [venue name] last night. I had a fantastic time and appreciated the opportunity to share my music with your audience. I'd love to stay in touch for any future events. Thanks again for all your support!

Best,
[Your Name]"

Conclusion

EFFECTIVE COMMUNICATION is the backbone of successful gig booking. By being clear, respectful, and professional in your interactions with venues, you can troubleshoot common issues and improve your booking process. Remember, every gig is not just an opportunity to perform, but also to build lasting relationships in the music industry. With the right approach, you'll not only secure more gigs but also create a reputation as a reliable and professional artist.

Fan Engagement Strategies for Authentic Connection

In the fast-paced, ever-evolving world of music, building a strong and loyal fanbase is more critical than ever. However, the key to not just gaining fans but keeping them engaged lies in the authenticity of your interactions. This is the art of fan engagement strategies, a puzzle that many artists struggle to solve. But fear not! With the right strategies, you can connect with your fans in a meaningful and lasting way. Here's how:

1. Know Your Audience

UNDERSTANDING YOUR audience is the first step to authentic engagement. Take the time to learn who your fans are—what they like, what they value, and how they interact online. Use analytics tools to track demographics, engagement patterns, and feedback. This information will help you tailor your content and communication style to resonate with your fans' needs and preferences.

2. Be Genuine in Your Communication

FANS CAN TELL WHEN an artist is being inauthentic. Whether you're posting on social media, responding to comments, or engaging in live streams, make sure your interactions are sincere. Share your true thoughts, experiences, and feelings. Authenticity builds trust, and trust fosters loyalty.

3. Share Behind-the-Scenes Content

PEOPLE LOVE GETTING a peek behind the curtain. Share snippets of your life as an artist—whether it's the creative process, rehearsals, or just a day in the life. This kind of content makes fans feel like they're part of your journey, deepening their connection to you and your music.

4. Respond to Your Fans

ONE OF THE MOST EFFECTIVE ways to engage with your fans is by acknowledging them. Reply to comments, like posts where you're tagged, and show appreciation for fan art or covers. Even a simple "thank you" can make a fan feel valued and more connected to you.

5. Host Interactive Events

LIVE STREAMS, Q&A SESSIONS, and virtual meet-and-greets are fantastic ways to engage directly with your fans. These events create a two-way conversation, allowing you to interact with your audience in real-time. They also provide an opportunity for fans to ask questions, offer feedback, and feel more involved in your journey.

6. Incorporate Fan Feedback

LISTENING TO YOUR FANS and incorporating their feedback shows that you value their opinions. Whether it's about a new song, a piece of merch, or even tour locations, taking their suggestions into account can make them feel like they're part of the creative process.

7. Create a Community

BUILDING A COMMUNITY around your music is a powerful way to keep fans engaged. Encourage fans to connect with each other through your social media platforms, fan clubs, or online forums. A strong, connected fan community can sustain itself, with fans keeping each other excited and engaged, even when you're not actively promoting something.

8. Give Back to Your Fans

OFFER EXCLUSIVE CONTENT, early access to new music, or limited-edition merchandise as a way to reward your most loyal fans. These gestures of appreciation can go a long way in building a dedicated fanbase. Moreover, when fans feel appreciated, they're more likely to stick around and continue supporting your career.

9. Be Consistent

CONSISTENCY IS KEY to maintaining fan engagement. Regular updates, consistent communication, and ongoing interaction keep your fans invested. Whether you're releasing new music, sharing updates, or simply interacting on social media, make sure you're consistent in your presence and engagement.

10. Stay True to Your Art

LASTLY, NEVER LOSE sight of your music and what makes you unique. Fans are drawn to your authenticity and creativity, so stay true to your artistic vision. When your art is genuine, the connection with your fans will naturally follow.

Conclusion

SOLVING THE FAN ENGAGEMENT puzzle is not about following a rigid formula but about connecting authentically with your audience. By understanding your fans, communicating sincerely, and consistently engaging with them, you can build a loyal fanbase that grows with you throughout your career. Remember, at the heart of it all is the music and the unique bond you create with those who love it.

Effective Band Bios: Crafting Compelling Artist Stories

A well-crafted band bio is more than just a collection of facts; it's a story that captures the essence of who you are as a group and what you stand for. Whether you're a new band looking to make your mark or an established act seeking to refresh your image, a compelling band bio is crucial for connecting with fans, promoters, and industry professionals. Here's how to craft a compelling artist story that resonates.

1. Know Your Audience

BEFORE YOU START WRITING, consider who will be reading your bio. Are you targeting fans, press, venue owners, or record labels? Each audience might be looking for something slightly different, so tailor your bio to meet their needs.

Tip: For a general band bio, aim for a balance that appeals to all potential readers. If you're writing for a specific purpose, such as submitting to a festival, emphasize elements that align with that event's vibe or audience.

2. Start with a Strong Hook

THE OPENING OF YOUR bio should grab the reader's attention. Think of it as the first impression you make on someone who knows nothing about your band. A compelling hook could be an intriguing fact, a memorable quote, or a bold statement about your music.

Example: "Born in the heart of the city and raised on the raw energy of the underground scene, [Band Name] delivers a sonic experience that's as gritty as it is exhilarating."

3. Tell Your Story

EVERY BAND HAS A STORY, and this is the heart of your bio. How did you come together? What drives your music? What challenges have you overcome? Your story should reflect your band's personality, values, and journey, making it relatable and engaging.

   Tip: Focus on what makes your band unique. Whether it's your origin story, the diversity of your influences, or your mission as a group, highlight the elements that set you apart from other bands.

4. Highlight Key Achievements

WHILE YOUR BIO SHOULD be narrative-driven, it's also important to include your band's accomplishments. This could be anything from releasing an album, playing at notable venues, winning awards, or collaborating with other artists. These achievements lend credibility and show that you're serious about your craft.

   Tip: Be selective and concise. Highlight the most impressive and relevant achievements without overwhelming the reader with too much information.

5. Describe Your Sound

YOUR MUSIC IS, OF COURSE, the core of your band's identity. But describing music can be tricky, especially if your sound doesn't fit neatly into a single genre. Use vivid, descriptive language to convey the essence of your sound, and don't be afraid to reference other artists or genres to give readers a point of reference.

   Example: "With soaring vocals, intricate guitar work, and a rhythm section that grooves like no other, [Band Name] blends the anthemic energy of classic rock with the introspective depth of indie folk."

6. Show Your Personality

YOUR BIO IS AN OPPORTUNITY to show off your band's personality. Whether you're edgy and rebellious, laid-back and fun, or deeply introspective, let that shine through in your writing. This helps to create a connection with readers who share similar vibes or values.

Tip: Incorporate humor, wit, or emotion where appropriate, but keep it authentic. Forced humor or exaggerated claims can come off as insincere.

7. Keep It Concise and Readable

ATTENTION SPANS ARE short, especially in today's digital age. Your band bio should be engaging but also to the point. Aim for a length of around 250-400 words for a standard bio. Use short paragraphs, bullet points, or headings to break up the text and make it more digestible.

Tip: After writing your bio, step away from it for a bit, then return with fresh eyes to edit and trim any unnecessary details. Make sure every word serves a purpose.

8. Include a Call to Action

WHILE THE PRIMARY PURPOSE of your bio is to inform and engage, it's also a good idea to direct readers to where they can hear your music, follow you on social media, or get in touch for bookings. A simple call to action at the end of your bio can guide them to the next step.

Example: "Check out [Band Name]'s latest single on Spotify, and follow them on Instagram for updates on new releases and upcoming shows."

Final Thoughts

CRAFTING AN EFFECTIVE band bio is both an art and a science. It requires a balance of storytelling, factual information, and personality to create a narrative that truly represents your band. Remember, your bio is often the first impression someone will have of your group, so make it count. With these tips in mind, you can create a compelling artist story that resonates with your audience and leaves a lasting impression.

Success With Music Collaboration: Overcoming Communication Challenges

Collaboration is a powerful tool in the creative world, often leading to innovative and exciting projects that push the boundaries of what's possible. However, working with other artists isn't always smooth sailing. Communication challenges can arise, and if not addressed, they can derail even the most promising collaborations. Whether you're working on a song, an album, or a multimedia project, here are some tips to ensure your success with music collaboration by overcoming communication challenges.

1. Establish Clear Goals from the Start

ONE OF THE MOST COMMON communication challenges in collaboration is a lack of clarity around the project's goals. Before diving into the creative process, it's crucial to have a discussion about what each party hopes to achieve. Are you aiming for a particular sound, message, or style? Understanding each other's vision can prevent misunderstandings down the line and keep everyone focused on the same end goal.

Tip: Create a shared document where everyone can jot down their ideas, goals, and expectations for the project. Revisit this document regularly to ensure everyone is still on the same page.

2. Define Roles and Responsibilities

ANOTHER COMMON PITFALL in collaborations is the ambiguity around roles and responsibilities. Who's in charge of what? Who has the final say in creative decisions? Defining roles early on

BRANDING & NETWORKING SUCCESS FOR BANDS

can prevent conflicts and ensure that each artist can focus on their strengths.

Tip: Have an open discussion about each person's role in the project. Whether you're co-writing, producing, or performing, understanding who is responsible for each aspect will streamline the process and reduce potential friction.

3. Practice Active Listening

EFFECTIVE COMMUNICATION is as much about listening as it is about talking. Active listening involves fully concentrating, understanding, responding, and then remembering what the other person says. It's important to make sure that everyone involved in the collaboration feels heard and respected.

Tip: When discussing ideas, avoid interrupting and make a conscious effort to understand the other person's perspective. Repeat back what you've heard to confirm understanding before responding.

4. Be Open to Feedback

CREATIVITY OFTEN INVOLVES personal expression, which can make receiving feedback challenging. However, constructive feedback is essential for growth and collaboration. Learning to give and receive feedback graciously can prevent communication breakdowns and lead to a stronger final product.

Tip: Frame feedback in a positive light, focusing on how suggestions can improve the project rather than criticizing what's wrong. Likewise, when receiving feedback, try to view it as an opportunity to refine and enhance your work.

5. Address Conflicts Early

CONFLICTS ARE ALMOST inevitable in any collaboration, but how they're handled can make or break the project. Ignoring or avoiding conflicts can lead to resentment and a breakdown in communication. It's better to address issues as they arise, with a focus on finding a resolution that works for everyone.

Tip: Approach conflicts with a problem-solving mindset. Instead of placing blame, focus on understanding the root of the issue and brainstorm possible solutions together. Keep the discussion respectful and centered on the project's success.

6. Use the Right Tools for Communication

IN TODAY'S DIGITAL age, there are countless tools available to facilitate communication and collaboration. Choosing the right tools can make a significant difference in how smoothly the collaboration runs. Whether it's for file sharing, video conferencing, or project management, having a centralized platform for communication can reduce misunderstandings and keep everyone organized.

Tip: Agree on the tools you'll use from the beginning, whether it's a messaging app like Slack, a file-sharing service like Google Drive, or a project management tool like Trello. Make sure everyone is comfortable using the chosen tools and that all communication is documented for future reference.

7. Maintain Regular Check-Ins

REGULAR COMMUNICATION is key to a successful collaboration. Even if things are going well, regular check-ins can help catch potential issues before they become problems. It also provides an opportunity to reassess goals, timelines, and the overall direction of the project.

Tip: Schedule regular meetings or check-ins to discuss progress, share updates, and address any concerns. Consistent communication helps maintain momentum and ensures everyone stays engaged and aligned.

8. Respect Each Other's Creative Process

EVERY ARTIST HAS THEIR own way of working, and these differences can sometimes lead to friction. Respecting each other's creative processes, even when they differ from your own, is crucial for a harmonious collaboration. Flexibility and understanding are key to making these differences work to your advantage.

Tip: Discuss your creative processes and preferences early on. If someone needs more time to work on their part or prefers to work in a certain environment, try to accommodate these needs as much as possible.

Final Thoughts

SUCCESSFUL COLLABORATION is all about communication, understanding, and mutual respect. By establishing clear goals, defining roles, practicing active listening, and using the right tools, you can overcome common communication challenges and create something truly special together. Remember, the strength of a collaboration lies in the diversity of ideas and the ability to merge them into a cohesive whole. With these tips in mind, you'll be well on your way to collaborative success.

Fan Feedback: Handling Criticism and Building Resilience

As a musician, fan feedback is an inevitable part of your journey. Whether it's praise for your latest release or constructive criticism of a live performance, how you handle feedback can significantly impact your growth as an artist and your relationship with your audience. While positive comments are always welcome, it's the negative or critical feedback that often challenges your confidence and resilience. This blog post explores how to manage fan feedback constructively, handle criticism gracefully, and build the resilience needed to thrive in the music industry.

The Importance of Fan Feedback

FAN FEEDBACK IS A VALUABLE resource for musicians. It provides insight into how your music resonates with your audience and can guide your creative decisions. Here's why it's important to pay attention to what your fans are saying:

1. Understanding Audience Preferences:

Feedback helps you understand what your fans love about your music and what they might want more (or less) of. This can inform your future projects and help you stay connected to your audience's evolving tastes.

2. Personal and Professional Growth:

Constructive criticism offers an opportunity for growth. It highlights areas where you can improve and challenges you to refine your craft, making you a better musician.

3. Strengthening Fan Relationships:

Engaging with fan feedback—whether positive or negative—shows that you value your audience's opinions. This interaction can strengthen your connection with fans and foster a loyal community around your music.

Handling Criticism Gracefully

CRITICISM CAN BE DIFFICULT to accept, especially when you've put your heart and soul into your work. However, how you respond to criticism can either build or undermine your credibility as an artist. Here's how to handle criticism gracefully:

1. Separate Yourself from Your Work

It's important to remember that criticism of your music is not a personal attack. Your art is an expression of your creativity, but it doesn't define your worth as a person. By distancing yourself from your work, you can evaluate feedback more objectively.

- Don't Take It Personally: Understand that not everyone will connect with your music in the same way. Negative feedback is often a reflection of personal taste rather than a judgment of your talent.

- Focus on the Message, Not the Tone: Sometimes criticism is delivered harshly. Instead of reacting to the tone, try to extract the constructive elements of the feedback. What can you learn from it?

2. Respond with Gratitude

When faced with criticism, your first instinct might be to defend yourself or dismiss the feedback. Instead, take a moment to express gratitude.

- Thank the Critic: A simple "Thank you for your feedback" can go a long way. It shows that you are open to different perspectives and willing to engage in a constructive dialogue.

- Acknowledge Valid Points: If the criticism is valid, acknowledge it. For example, if a fan points out a flaw in your performance, you might say, "I appreciate you bringing this to my attention, and I'll work on improving that aspect."

3. Reflect Before Responding

It's natural to feel defensive when receiving criticism, but responding impulsively can lead to unnecessary conflict. Instead, take time to reflect on the feedback before you respond.

- Pause and Breathe: If you're feeling upset, take a break before responding. This gives you time to calm down and approach the situation with a clear mind.

- Consider the Source: Not all criticism is equally valuable. Consider the source of the feedback—are they a long-time fan, a fellow musician, or someone with little knowledge of your genre? This can help you decide how much weight to give their opinion.

4. Engage Constructively

Engaging constructively with critics can turn a negative situation into a positive one. It can lead to meaningful conversations that benefit both you and your fans.

- Ask for Specifics: If the criticism is vague, ask for more details. For example, if someone says they didn't like a song, you could ask, "What specifically didn't work for you?" This can provide you with actionable insights.

- Offer Your Perspective: While it's important to listen, it's also okay to share your perspective. You might explain your artistic choices or the context behind a particular decision. Just be sure to do so respectfully and without sounding defensive.

Building Resilience in the Face of Criticism

DEVELOPING RESILIENCE is crucial for long-term success in the music industry. Resilience allows you to bounce back from setbacks, maintain your passion for music, and continue growing as an artist. Here's how to build resilience when dealing with criticism:

1. Embrace a Growth Mindset

A growth mindset is the belief that your abilities and talents can be developed through effort and learning. This mindset helps you view criticism as an opportunity for improvement rather than a threat.

- See Criticism as Feedback, Not Failure: Instead of viewing criticism as a reflection of your shortcomings, see it as valuable feedback that can help you grow.

- Learn from Mistakes: Mistakes are an inevitable part of the creative process. Embrace them as learning opportunities and use them to refine your skills.

2. Surround Yourself with Support

Having a strong support system can help you stay grounded and resilient in the face of criticism.

- Seek Out Constructive Critique: Surround yourself with people who give you honest, constructive feedback. This could be fellow musicians, mentors, or trusted friends. Their input can help you improve without feeling discouraged.

- Lean on Your Community: When you're feeling down about negative feedback, reach out to your community of supporters. Their encouragement can remind you of your strengths and keep you motivated.

3. Focus on Your Vision

It's important to stay true to your artistic vision, even when faced with criticism. Remember why you started making music and what you want to achieve.

- Set Personal Goals: Set goals that align with your vision and measure your success by your own standards, not by the opinions of others.

- Stay Passionate: Keep your passion for music alive by focusing on the aspects of your work that bring you joy. Passion fuels resilience and helps you push through challenges.

4. Practice Self-Care

Taking care of your mental and emotional well-being is essential for building resilience.

- Take Breaks: If criticism is overwhelming, it's okay to take a step back and focus on self-care. Spend time doing things you enjoy outside of music to recharge your energy.

- Develop Healthy Coping Strategies: Find healthy ways to cope with stress and criticism, such as exercise, meditation, or talking to a therapist. These strategies can help you maintain a positive mindset.

Conclusion

FAN FEEDBACK IS AN integral part of your journey as a musician. While criticism can be challenging, handling it with grace and building resilience can help you grow as an artist and strengthen your connection with your audience. By embracing a growth mindset, surrounding yourself with support, staying true to your vision, and practicing self-care, you can navigate feedback constructively and continue to thrive in your musical career. Remember, every piece of feedback—positive or negative—is an opportunity to learn, grow, and become the best version of yourself as an artist.

Tips to Enhance Content Virality

In the digital age, creating content that resonates with your audience is essential, but creating content that people want to share is the holy grail of online marketing. Whether you're a blogger, brand, or content creator, cracking the virality code can exponentially increase your reach and influence. But what makes content shareworthy? And how can you create pieces that have the potential to go viral? Let's dive into the strategies for solving the virality equation and crafting content that your audience can't resist sharing with "Tips to Enhance Content Virality."

Understanding Virality: The Basics

VIRALITY IS WHEN CONTENT spreads rapidly from person to person, often across social media platforms, reaching a massive audience in a short amount of time. But virality isn't just about luck—it's about tapping into the elements that make people want to share.

To create shareable content, you need to understand the psychology behind why people share. Research shows that people share content for several key reasons:

1. To Entertain or Amuse: People love sharing content that makes them laugh or feel good.
2. To Inform or Educate: Content that offers valuable information or new insights is often shared.
3. To Express Identity: People share content that reflects their beliefs, values, or identity.
4. To Build Relationships: Sharing content can be a way to connect with others and foster relationships.
5. To Show Support: Content that aligns with a cause or movement often garners shares from those who want to show their support.

Strategies for Creating Shareable Content

1. CRAFT COMPELLING Headlines
- Hook Your Audience: Your headline is the first impression. It needs to be catchy, intriguing, and promise value. Use numbers, questions, or emotional triggers to draw readers in. For example, "10 Simple Habits That Will Change Your Life" or "Are You Making These Common Mistakes?"
- Optimize for SEO: While crafting an engaging headline, don't forget to incorporate relevant keywords. This not only helps with search engine rankings but also increases the likelihood of your content being discovered and shared.

2. Tap Into Emotions
- Evoke Strong Feelings: Content that evokes strong emotions—whether it's joy, anger, surprise, or sadness—tends to be more shareable. Emotional content connects with people on a deeper level, prompting them to share with others who might feel the same way.
- Use Storytelling: Stories are powerful because they make information relatable and memorable. Whether you're sharing a personal experience, a customer success story, or a narrative that supports your brand, storytelling can make your content more engaging and shareworthy.

3. Create Value-Rich Content
- Offer Practical Tips: Content that provides actionable advice or practical tips is highly shareable. People love sharing content that makes them look knowledgeable or helpful to their peers.
- Provide In-Depth Analysis: Comprehensive guides, detailed tutorials, and in-depth analyses are often seen as valuable resources worth sharing. Invest time in creating content that is informative, well-researched, and offers unique insights.

4. Make It Visually Appealing

- Use High-Quality Images and Videos: Visual content is more likely to be shared than text-only content. Use eye-catching images, infographics, and videos to complement your message and make it more engaging.

- Design for Easy Sharing: Ensure your visuals are optimized for social media platforms. Use the right dimensions, include captions, and make sure your branding is clear. A well-designed image or video is more likely to be shared.

5. Incorporate Social Proof

- Highlight User-Generated Content: Sharing testimonials, reviews, or content created by your audience can increase trust and encourage others to share. People are more likely to share content that others have already endorsed.

- Showcase Numbers: If your content has already been shared widely or viewed many times, highlight these numbers. Social proof can drive more people to share your content, as it signals popularity and credibility.

6. Make Sharing Easy

- Add Social Sharing Buttons: Place social sharing buttons prominently on your website, blog, and emails. Make it as easy as possible for readers to share your content with a single click.

- Optimize for Mobile: Ensure that your content is mobile-friendly. With the majority of content consumption happening on mobile devices, your content must be easy to read, view, and share on smaller screens.

7. Leverage Trending Topics

- Tap into Current Events: Create content that aligns with trending topics or current events. Content that is timely and relevant is more likely to be shared, especially if it offers a fresh perspective on a popular subject.

- Use Hashtags: Incorporate relevant hashtags into your social media posts to increase the discoverability of your content. Hashtags can help you tap into ongoing conversations and make your content more visible to a wider audience.

8. Engage with Your Audience

- Encourage Participation: Invite your audience to engage with your content by asking questions, running polls, or encouraging them to share their thoughts. Content that sparks conversation is more likely to be shared.

- Respond and Interact: Engage with your audience by responding to comments, sharing user-generated content, and participating in discussions. Building a strong connection with your audience can lead to more shares.

9. Experiment with Content Formats

- Diversify Your Content: Experiment with different content formats like quizzes, memes, challenges, and interactive posts. Different formats appeal to different audiences, and some may be more likely to go viral than others.

- Repurpose Content: Turn a blog post into an infographic, a video into a podcast, or a tweet into a longer article. Repurposing content in various formats can increase its shareability and reach.

10. Analyze and Adapt

- Monitor Performance: Use analytics tools to track the performance of your content. Pay attention to metrics like shares, likes, comments, and engagement rates to understand what works best.

- Refine Your Strategy: Based on your findings, refine your content strategy. Focus on the types of content that resonate most with your audience and lead to the highest shares.

Conclusion

CREATING SHAREABLE content is both an art and a science. While there's no guaranteed formula for virality, understanding the elements that make content shareworthy can significantly

increase your chances of reaching a broader audience. By crafting compelling headlines, tapping into emotions, offering valuable insights, and making it easy for your audience to share, you can create content that not only resonates but also spreads like wildfire across the digital landscape.

Start applying these strategies today, and you might just find that solving the virality equation is within your reach.

Creating Engaging Instagram Stories: Troubleshooting Tips & Optimization Strategies

Instagram Stories have become a powerful tool for personal branding, businesses, and content creators to engage with their audience. They offer a unique way to connect through visuals, videos, polls, and interactive elements. However, creating engaging stories isn't always straightforward. Here's a guide to troubleshooting common issues and optimizing your Instagram Stories to captivate your audience.

Why Instagram Stories Matter

INSTAGRAM STORIES ARE more than just fleeting images or videos—they're a way to tell a story, build a brand, and foster a deeper connection with your followers. With over 500 million users engaging with Stories daily, the potential reach is enormous. The trick is to make your content stand out amidst the sea of other stories.

Troubleshooting Common Issues

1. LOW ENGAGEMENT RATES
 - Problem: Your Stories aren't getting the views, likes, or responses you hoped for.
 - Solution: Analyze your content. Are you posting at the right time? Consider your audience's peak activity hours. Use Instagram's insights to determine when your followers are most active and tailor your posting schedule accordingly. Also, experiment with different formats—photos, videos, boomerangs, and polls—to see what resonates most with your audience.

BRANDING & NETWORKING SUCCESS FOR BANDS

2. Blurry Images or Videos
- Problem: Your images or videos appear blurry or low quality.
- Solution: This could be due to Instagram's compression or uploading lower resolution content. Always upload photos with a resolution of 1080x1920 pixels, which is Instagram's preferred size for Stories. For videos, use a high-resolution file (no larger than 15MB) and avoid editing or compressing them in third-party apps before uploading.

3. Sound Issues
- Problem: Audio doesn't play correctly in your Stories.
- Solution: Ensure that your phone's sound is on and the volume is turned up. If the issue persists, try restarting the app or updating to the latest version of Instagram. Sometimes, the problem could be with the video file itself; in such cases, try re-uploading the content.

4. Story Won't Upload
- Problem: Your Story gets stuck or fails to upload.
- Solution: Check your internet connection—stories require a stable connection for upload. If your connection is fine, try closing and reopening the app, or restarting your phone. Clear the app cache or update Instagram to the latest version to resolve any underlying software bugs.

Optimization Strategies for Better Engagement

1. USE INTERACTIVE Features
- Polls, Quizzes, and Questions: These features invite your audience to participate actively in your Stories. They're not only fun but also provide valuable insights into your followers' preferences.
- Countdowns and Stickers: Use countdowns for upcoming events or product launches to build anticipation. Stickers can make your stories more visually appealing and engaging.

2. Leverage User-Generated Content

- Share content created by your followers. This not only builds community but also encourages others to create content featuring your brand.

3. Tell a Story

- Don't just post random images or videos; create a narrative. Whether it's a day in the life, behind-the-scenes content, or a tutorial, make sure your story has a beginning, middle, and end. This keeps viewers hooked and encourages them to watch till the last slide.

4. Incorporate Branding

- Use consistent fonts, colors, and styles that align with your brand. This creates a cohesive look and makes your stories instantly recognizable.

5. Utilize Analytics

- Instagram Insights can show you how your stories are performing. Pay attention to metrics like reach, impressions, and exit rates. Adjust your strategy based on what's working and what's not. For example, if you notice a high exit rate on certain types of content, consider changing your approach.

6. Experiment with Different Content Types

- Try different formats: live videos, boomerangs, GIFs, and even user polls. Diversifying your content keeps your audience engaged and can help you discover what they enjoy most.

Conclusion

CREATING ENGAGING INSTAGRAM Stories is both an art and a science. While it's essential to be creative and original, you also need to pay attention to the technical aspects that can affect your story's performance. By troubleshooting common issues and implementing these optimization strategies, you can enhance the impact of your Instagram Stories, grow your audience, and build stronger connections with your followers.

Start experimenting today, and watch your engagement soar!

Building Your Email Fanbase: Effective Email Marketing Strategies to Engage Your Audience

In today's digital age, building a fanbase as a musician, artist, or content creator requires more than just talent and creativity. While social media is a powerful tool for reaching new audiences, email marketing remains one of the most effective ways to engage and nurture your existing fanbase. With the right strategies, email campaigns can help you build stronger relationships with your fans, keep them informed about your latest projects, and turn casual listeners into loyal supporters. Here's how to harness the power of email marketing to grow and sustain your fanbase.

1. Why Email Marketing Matters for Building a Fanbase

EMAIL MARKETING OFFERS a level of direct communication that social media platforms simply can't match. When someone subscribes to your email list, they're inviting you into their personal inbox, giving you a direct line to their attention. Unlike social media algorithms that can hide your posts from followers, email ensures your message reaches your fans. Additionally, email marketing allows for more personalized and targeted communication, which is key to building deeper connections with your audience.

2. Start with a Solid Foundation: Build Your Email List

YOUR EMAIL MARKETING efforts are only as strong as your email list. Start by building a list of fans who are genuinely interested in your work.

- Offer Value in Exchange for Emails: Encourage fans to join your email list by offering something valuable in return. This could be a free download of your latest single, exclusive access to behind-the-scenes content, or early access to tickets for your next show.

- Promote Your Email List on Social Media: Use your social media platforms to promote your email list. Highlight the benefits of subscribing and make it easy for your followers to sign up by including direct links to your signup form.

- Use Your Website: Make sure your website has prominent sign-up forms. Consider adding pop-ups or banners that invite visitors to join your mailing list, and emphasize the benefits they'll receive by subscribing.

3. Craft Engaging and Personalized Content

ONCE YOU'VE BUILT YOUR email list, the next step is to create content that engages your audience and keeps them coming back for more.

- Segment Your Audience: Not all your fans are the same, so segment your email list based on factors like location, engagement level, or interests. This allows you to send more relevant content to each group. For example, fans in a specific city could receive updates about upcoming concerts in their area, while others might get news about new releases.

- Tell Your Story: Use your emails to share your journey, the story behind your music, or the creative process behind your projects. Fans love to feel connected to the artists they support, and sharing personal stories helps build that connection.

- Incorporate Visuals: Make your emails visually appealing by incorporating images, videos, and graphics. Use album artwork, concert photos, or short video clips to capture attention and make your emails stand out in crowded inboxes.

4. Keep Your Audience Informed and Excited

REGULARLY UPDATE YOUR fans with relevant news and exciting announcements to keep them engaged and eager to open your emails.

- Exclusive Content: Reward your email subscribers with content they can't find anywhere else. This could be sneak peeks of new music, early access to tickets, or exclusive merchandise. Making your subscribers feel like insiders encourages them to stay on your list and remain engaged.
- Regular Newsletters: Consider sending out a monthly or bi-weekly newsletter that includes updates on your latest projects, upcoming events, and recent achievements. Consistency is key to maintaining engagement, so establish a regular schedule and stick to it.
- Call to Action: Every email should have a clear call to action (CTA), whether it's inviting your fans to listen to your new single, watch your latest music video, or purchase tickets to an upcoming show. Make your CTAs stand out by using buttons or links that are easy to click.

5. Leverage Automation to Streamline Your Campaigns

AUTOMATION CAN SAVE you time and ensure that your fans receive timely and relevant content.

- Welcome Series: Set up an automated welcome series that introduces new subscribers to your music and your brand. This series could include a welcome email, a behind-the-scenes look at your creative process, and a special offer like a discount on merchandise.
- Drip Campaigns: Use drip campaigns to nurture relationships with your fans over time. For example, you could create a series of emails that gradually introduce your fans to your discography, with each email highlighting a different album or single.

- Birthday and Anniversary Emails: Send automated birthday or anniversary emails with special offers or exclusive content to celebrate these milestones with your fans.

6. Measure Your Success and Optimize Your Strategy

TO ENSURE YOUR EMAIL marketing efforts are effective, regularly track your performance and make adjustments as needed.
- Open Rates and Click-Through Rates: Monitor your open rates and click-through rates to gauge how well your emails are performing. Low open rates may indicate that your subject lines need improvement, while low click-through rates could suggest that your content or CTAs aren't resonating with your audience.
- A/B Testing: Experiment with different elements of your emails, such as subject lines, content formats, or send times, to see what resonates best with your audience. A/B testing allows you to compare different versions of an email and choose the one that performs better.
- Gather Feedback: Don't be afraid to ask your fans for feedback on your emails. A simple survey or a direct question in your email can provide valuable insights into what your audience likes and what they'd like to see more of.

7. Build Long-Term Relationships with Your Fans

EMAIL MARKETING ISN'T just about promoting your latest project; it's about building long-term relationships with your fans.
- Show Appreciation: Regularly thank your subscribers for their support. A simple message of gratitude or a special offer can go a long way in making your fans feel valued.
- Engage Personally: Occasionally send personalized emails or respond directly to fan replies. This level of personal engagement can deepen the connection between you and your audience.

- Consistency Over Time: Building a loyal fanbase takes time, so be patient and consistent with your email marketing efforts. Keep your audience engaged with regular, meaningful communication, and over time, you'll see your fanbase grow.

Conclusion

EMAIL MARKETING IS a powerful tool for building and engaging a loyal fanbase. By offering value, crafting engaging content, and leveraging automation, you can create effective email campaigns that keep your fans excited and connected to your music or content. Remember, the key to successful email marketing is building relationships—so focus on providing value, showing appreciation, and maintaining consistent communication with your audience. With these strategies in place, you'll be well on your way to growing a dedicated and engaged fanbase.

Creating a Killer EPK: Essential Elements and Troubleshooting

In the music and entertainment industry, first impressions are everything, and nothing makes a better first impression than a killer Electronic Press Kit (EPK). Whether you're an emerging artist, a seasoned band, or a professional in any creative field, an EPK is your golden ticket to capturing attention, securing gigs, and elevating your brand. But what exactly goes into creating an EPK that stands out from the crowd? In this article, we'll break down the essential elements and guide you through the process of building an impressive EPK, while also troubleshooting common issues you might encounter along the way.

What is an EPK?

AN ELECTRONIC PRESS Kit, or EPK, is a digital portfolio that provides the media, booking agents, and other industry professionals with everything they need to know about you. Think of it as your online resume, but with more flair and multimedia elements that showcase your talent and personality.

In the past, artists and bands would send physical press kits to media outlets, containing printed bios, photos, and CDs. With the rise of digital media, EPKs have become the standard, allowing for instant sharing and access to your materials anytime, anywhere.

Why Do You Need a Killer EPK?

HAVING A WELL-CRAFTED EPK is crucial for several reasons:
 - Professionalism: An EPK presents you as a serious artist or professional who is ready for business.

- Accessibility: It allows industry professionals to quickly access and share your information.

- Brand Building: A killer EPK helps you control your narrative and brand image.

- Time-Saving: With all your materials in one place, you save time when pitching yourself to potential clients or media outlets.

Essential Elements of an EPK

BIOGRAPHY

Your biography is the heart of your EPK. It tells your story, highlights your achievements, and gives a personal touch that connects with the reader. Whether you're an artist, band, or professional, your bio should be concise yet compelling. Include key milestones, influences, and what sets you apart in your field.

High-Quality Media

Visuals are a powerful tool in your EPK. Professional photos, album covers, and logos create a strong visual identity. If you're a musician, including video content like music videos or live performances is a must. This allows industry professionals to see and hear you in action.

Discography or Portfolio

This section is where you showcase your work. For musicians, this means listing albums, singles, and notable collaborations. If you're in another field, include a portfolio of your best projects. Organize this content in a way that's easy to navigate, making sure your most impressive work is front and center.

Press Clippings and Reviews

Positive press and reviews can add significant weight to your EPK. Include snippets of articles, interviews, and reviews that highlight your work. If you're just starting and don't have much press coverage, consider including testimonials from fans or clients.

Contact Information

Make it easy for people to reach you. Include your email, phone number, and links to your social media profiles. If you have a manager or publicist, be sure to include their contact details as well.

Tour Dates and Event Information

If you're a performing artist, this section is essential. Keep your tour dates, upcoming shows, and events up-to-date. This not only informs your audience but can also help you book more gigs by showing your active schedule.

Branding and Design

Your EPK should reflect your brand's identity. Use consistent colors, fonts, and imagery that match your other promotional materials. A well-designed EPK creates a memorable impression and sets you apart from others.

Building Your EPK: Step-by-Step Guide

CHOOSING THE RIGHT Platform

Decide whether you want a hosted EPK (on platforms like Sonicbids or ReverbNation) or a self-hosted EPK on your website. Each option has its pros and cons, depending on your needs and budget.

Designing Your EPK

Focus on creating a user-friendly layout that's easy to navigate. A clean, organized design will keep the viewer engaged. Don't forget to make your EPK mobile-responsive, as many people will view it on their phones.

Writing and Editing Content

The content in your EPK should be clear, concise, and free of errors. Write in a way that's engaging and professional. Editing is crucial – ensure everything is polished before you share your EPK with the world.

Troubleshooting Common EPK Problems

TECHNICAL ISSUES

Broken links and missing files can ruin the effectiveness of your EPK. Regularly check your EPK to ensure all links are working and files are properly uploaded.

Outdated Content

Keeping your EPK current is vital. Update it regularly with new photos, press clippings, and tour dates to reflect your latest achievements.

Lack of Engagement

If your EPK isn't generating the response you hoped for, consider adding more interactive elements like videos or links to your social media. Engaging content can make a big difference.

Conclusion

CREATING A KILLER EPK is about more than just putting together a few photos and a bio. It's about telling your story in a way that resonates with industry professionals and showcases your unique talents. By including all the essential elements and keeping your EPK up-to-date, you'll be well on your way to making a lasting impression.

FAQs

1. HOW OFTEN SHOULD I update my EPK?
 - You should update your EPK whenever there's a significant change, such as a new release, tour dates, or major press coverage. Aim to review and refresh your EPK at least every few months.
 2. Can I use a free platform to create my EPK?

- Yes, there are free platforms available, but they may come with limitations. A self-hosted EPK on your website offers more flexibility and control over your content and branding.

3. What should I do if I don't have any press clippings?

- If you lack press coverage, consider including testimonials from fans or industry peers. You can also focus on building this section over time as you gain more exposure.

4. How do I make my EPK stand out?

- Focus on high-quality visuals, a compelling bio, and engaging content. Make sure your EPK reflects your unique brand and personality.

5. Is it necessary to have both a website and an EPK?

- While not mandatory, having both a website and an EPK can be beneficial. Your website serves as a broader online presence, while your EPK is a targeted tool for media and industry professionals.

Live Streaming Hacks: Troubleshooting Livestream Issues

Live streaming has become a powerful tool for musicians, content creators, businesses, and anyone looking to connect with their audience in real-time. However, the success of a live stream can be quickly derailed by technical glitches. Nothing is more frustrating than buffering, poor audio quality, or sudden disconnects when you're trying to deliver a live performance or presentation. Fortunately, with the right preparation and troubleshooting livestream issues, you can minimize these issues and ensure a smooth, glitch-free live stream. Here are some essential hacks to keep your live stream running flawlessly.

1. Prepare Your Equipment and Setup

BEFORE YOU GO LIVE, it's crucial to ensure that your equipment and setup are optimized for streaming.

- Check Your Internet Connection: A strong, stable internet connection is the backbone of any live stream. Aim for an upload speed of at least 5 Mbps for standard definition streaming and 10 Mbps or higher for HD quality. Use a wired Ethernet connection instead of Wi-Fi to reduce the risk of drops in connection quality.

- Test Your Equipment: Before going live, thoroughly test your camera, microphone, and any other equipment. Ensure that your camera is producing a clear image, your microphone is capturing clean audio, and all connections are secure.

- Update Software and Firmware: Make sure that all your streaming software, camera, and audio equipment are up to date. Software updates often include bug fixes and performance improvements that can enhance your streaming experience.

2. Optimize Audio Quality

POOR AUDIO QUALITY is a major turnoff for viewers, even more so than low video quality. Here's how to ensure your sound is top-notch.

- Use an External Microphone: Built-in microphones on cameras or laptops often produce subpar audio. Invest in a good quality external microphone, whether it's a USB mic, a lavalier, or a professional condenser mic, to capture clear, crisp sound.

- Eliminate Background Noise: Stream from a quiet environment to minimize background noise. If noise is unavoidable, consider using noise-cancelling software or a microphone with a built-in noise reduction feature.

- Monitor Audio Levels: Use headphones to monitor your audio levels in real-time. This helps you catch and correct issues like clipping, distortion, or overly quiet sound before they ruin your stream.

3. Ensure Stable Video Quality

GLITCHES IN VIDEO QUALITY can distract your audience and make your stream difficult to watch.

- Adjust Bitrate Settings: Bitrate controls the quality of your video stream. If your stream is experiencing lag or buffering, consider lowering the bitrate. A lower bitrate requires less bandwidth and can help maintain a smoother stream.

- Choose the Right Resolution: Streaming at a resolution that your internet connection and equipment can't handle will result in dropped frames and poor video quality. Streaming in 720p is often a good balance between quality and stability if you're facing bandwidth limitations.

- Use a Backup Camera: If possible, have a second camera set up and ready to go in case your primary camera fails. Switching to a backup camera can save your stream if the primary camera encounters issues.

4. Optimize Your Streaming Software

YOUR STREAMING SOFTWARE is the control center for your live stream, so it's important to set it up correctly.

- Use a Reliable Streaming Platform: Whether you're using OBS, Streamlabs, or another software, make sure it's stable and well-suited to your needs. Test different platforms to see which works best with your hardware and streaming style.
- Set Up Scenes in Advance: If your stream involves multiple scenes (e.g., different camera angles, slideshows, or overlays), set them up in your streaming software beforehand. This minimizes the risk of mistakes or delays when switching between scenes during the live stream.
- Enable Stream Delay: If you're concerned about technical glitches or if your content is sensitive, enabling a short stream delay (5-10 seconds) can give you a buffer to address issues before they reach your audience.

5. Manage Your Resources

RESOURCE MANAGEMENT is key to preventing your computer from being overwhelmed during a live stream.

- Close Unnecessary Applications: Streaming is resource-intensive. Close any unnecessary programs or browser tabs to free up your computer's processing power and reduce the risk of your stream crashing.
- Monitor CPU and Memory Usage: Keep an eye on your CPU and memory usage during the stream. If either is consistently high,

consider lowering your stream quality or closing additional programs to prevent your system from overheating or freezing.

6. Prepare for Technical Difficulties

NO MATTER HOW WELL you prepare, technical difficulties can still arise. Have a plan in place to deal with them quickly.

- Have a Backup Plan: Create a backup plan for common issues. For example, if your internet connection drops, have a mobile hotspot ready to switch to. If your software crashes, know how to quickly reboot and resume your stream.
- Create a Technical Checklist: Before going live, go through a checklist to ensure everything is in order. This should include checking your internet connection, camera, microphone, streaming software, and any other equipment.
- Communicate with Your Audience: If technical issues do arise, communicate with your audience. Let them know what's happening and what you're doing to fix it. Transparency can help maintain viewer trust even in the face of problems.

7. Test Everything Before Going Live

ONE OF THE BEST WAYS to prevent technical glitches during your live stream is to conduct a thorough test run.

- Run a Private Test Stream: Set up a private or unlisted stream to test your entire setup. This allows you to check for potential issues without an audience and make necessary adjustments.
- Check for Latency: Latency can be an issue if you're interacting with your audience in real-time. Test the latency during your private stream and adjust settings to minimize delays.
- Simulate Real Conditions: Test your stream under the same conditions as your actual live stream. Use the same internet connection,

equipment, and streaming software to ensure that your test results are accurate.

8. Consider a Dedicated Streaming Setup

IF YOU'RE SERIOUS ABOUT live streaming, investing in a dedicated streaming setup can significantly reduce technical issues.
- Use a Streaming PC: A dedicated streaming PC, separate from your main computer, can handle the resource-heavy task of streaming. This reduces the strain on your primary computer and improves overall stability.
- Invest in a Capture Card: If you're streaming from a console or using a high-quality camera, a capture card can provide a stable, high-quality feed to your streaming software.
- Upgrade Your Internet Plan: If your current internet plan struggles to handle live streaming, consider upgrading to a plan with higher upload speeds and more reliable service.

Conclusion

LIVE STREAMING IS AN incredible way to connect with your audience in real-time, but technical glitches can quickly derail even the best-planned streams. By preparing your equipment, optimizing your setup, and having a plan in place to address potential issues, you can minimize disruptions and deliver a seamless live streaming experience. Remember, the key to a successful live stream is preparation, so take the time to test, troubleshoot, and optimize every aspect of your setup before going live. With these hacks, you'll be well on your way to glitch-free streaming and a more professional online presence.

SEO for Musicians: Boosting Website Visibility and Optimizing for Search Engines

In today's digital landscape, having a strong online presence is crucial for musicians. While social media and streaming platforms are essential, your website is the central hub where fans, industry professionals, and potential collaborators can learn more about you and your music. However, having a website isn't enough—you need to make sure it's discoverable. That's where Search Engine Optimization (SEO) comes in. Optimizing your website for search engines can significantly boost your visibility, driving more traffic and helping you reach a broader audience.

Why SEO Matters for Musicians

SEO IS THE PRACTICE of optimizing your website to rank higher in search engine results. When someone searches for a musician or music-related content, you want your site to appear at the top of the results. Higher rankings lead to more clicks, more engagement, and ultimately, more fans. With millions of websites competing for attention, effective SEO can make the difference between being discovered or overlooked.

Key SEO Strategies for Musicians

1. KEYWORD RESEARCH and Optimization
   - Understand Your Audience: Start by identifying the keywords your audience is using to search for music or artists like you. These could include your genre, similar artists, song titles, or even specific events.

- Incorporate Keywords: Use these keywords strategically throughout your website, including in your page titles, meta descriptions, headings, and content. For example, if you're a pop artist, phrases like "pop music artist," "new pop songs," or "indie pop musician" should be integrated naturally into your website text.

2. Optimize Your Website Content

- Create Quality Content: Regularly update your website with fresh content such as blog posts, news updates, tour dates, and new releases. Search engines favor websites that are consistently updated.

- Use Descriptive Text: For every page on your site, use descriptive text that clearly explains who you are and what you offer. Avoid generic language; be specific about your music, your brand, and what makes you unique.

- Optimize Media: Include alt text for images and videos, which helps search engines understand what the media is about. For example, if you post a picture from your latest gig, the alt text could be "Live performance by [Your Name] at [Venue]."

3. Improve Site Structure and Navigation

- User-Friendly Design: Ensure your website is easy to navigate. A well-organized site with clear menus helps both users and search engines find what they're looking for. Include sections for your bio, discography, tour dates, blog, and contact information.

- Internal Linking: Use internal links to connect your content. For example, if you write a blog post about your new album, link to the album's purchase or streaming page. This not only improves navigation but also helps search engines index your site more effectively.

4. Mobile Optimization

- Responsive Design: More than half of all web traffic comes from mobile devices, so it's crucial that your website is mobile-friendly. A responsive design ensures that your site looks and functions well on all devices, which is a factor search engines consider when ranking websites.

- Fast Loading Times: Optimize your website's loading speed by compressing images, reducing the use of heavy scripts, and using a reliable hosting service. Slow websites frustrate users and are penalized by search engines.

5. Build Backlinks

- Get Featured: Backlinks are links from other websites to yours, and they are a key factor in SEO. Reach out to music blogs, online magazines, and influencers to feature your music and link back to your site. Each backlink signals to search engines that your site is trustworthy and authoritative.

- Collaborate with Other Artists: Guest blog on another musician's site or collaborate on a project that links to your website. These collaborations can create valuable backlinks and introduce you to new audiences.

6. Leverage Social Media

- Promote Your Website: Use your social media platforms to drive traffic to your website. Share links to new blog posts, upcoming shows, or your latest music video. The more traffic you generate from social media, the better your SEO performance.

- Consistent Branding: Ensure that your social media profiles link back to your website and maintain consistent branding across all platforms. This builds brand recognition and improves your online presence.

7. Utilize Local SEO

- Optimize for Local Searches: If you perform live regularly or have a strong local following, optimizing for local SEO is essential. Include your location in your keywords and content, such as "Los Angeles indie musician" or "Nashville live music."

- Google My Business: Create a Google My Business profile to improve your visibility in local searches. This can help you appear in Google's local search results and on Google Maps, making it easier for fans to find your live shows or local events.

8. Monitor and Analyze Your Performance

- Use Analytics Tools: Tools like Google Analytics and Google Search Console provide insights into how visitors find and interact with your website. Track metrics like organic traffic, bounce rate, and keyword rankings to understand what's working and what needs improvement.

- Adjust Your Strategy: SEO is an ongoing process. Regularly review your analytics data to identify areas for improvement and adjust your strategy accordingly. Stay up-to-date with SEO trends and algorithm changes to maintain and improve your search engine rankings.

Conclusion

SEO IS A POWERFUL TOOL for musicians who want to boost their website visibility and reach a broader audience. By implementing these strategies, you can ensure that your site is not only user-friendly but also optimized for search engines. Remember, SEO is not a one-time task—it requires ongoing effort and adaptation to stay ahead of the competition. However, the payoff is worth it: increased traffic, more engaged fans, and greater opportunities to grow your music career.

Start optimizing your website today, and watch as your online presence—and your audience—begins to grow.

Social Media Algorithms Decoded: Understanding and Maximizing Your Reach

In the ever-evolving world of social media, understanding how algorithms work is crucial to maximizing your reach and ensuring that your content gets in front of the right audience. Whether you're an independent musician, a small business owner, or a content creator, deciphering these algorithms can feel like trying to crack a secret code. But fear not—this blog post will break down the basics of social media algorithms and provide actionable tips to help you leverage them effectively.

What Are Social Media Algorithms?

SOCIAL MEDIA ALGORITHMS are complex sets of rules and calculations used by platforms like Facebook, Instagram, Twitter, and TikTok to decide what content is shown to users and in what order. These algorithms analyze various factors to prioritize content that is most likely to engage each user, ensuring that they see the posts that are most relevant and interesting to them.

Each platform's algorithm works differently, but they all share a common goal: to keep users engaged on the platform by showing them content they will find valuable. Understanding the principles behind these algorithms can help you tailor your content strategy to increase visibility and engagement.

Key Factors That Influence Social Media Algorithms

WHILE EACH PLATFORM'S algorithm is unique, several key factors influence how content is ranked and displayed across the board.

1. Engagement: Engagement metrics—likes, comments, shares, and saves—are crucial indicators of how valuable and relevant your content is. The more engagement your posts receive, the more likely they are to be shown to a broader audience.

2. Relevance: Algorithms consider how relevant your content is to each user. This is determined by factors such as the user's past interactions with your profile, the types of content they usually engage with, and the keywords or hashtags you use.

3. Timeliness: Recent posts are often prioritized over older ones. Social media platforms want to show users the latest updates, so posting at optimal times when your audience is most active can boost your visibility.

4. Consistency: Regular posting signals to algorithms that your profile is active, which can positively impact your reach. Inconsistent posting, on the other hand, can lead to reduced visibility.

5. Content Type: Different content formats (videos, images, stories, live streams) are favored differently by each platform. For instance, Instagram's algorithm often prioritizes Reels and Stories, while Facebook gives more weight to live videos.

6. User Behavior: Algorithms take into account how users interact with the platform. If a user frequently engages with video content, for example, they're more likely to see videos in their feed.

Platform-Specific Algorithm Insights

LET'S DIVE DEEPER INTO how some of the most popular social media platforms' algorithms work and what you can do to maximize your reach on each.

1. Facebook

- Prioritize Quality Engagement: Facebook's algorithm values meaningful interactions, like comments and shares, more than passive likes. Encourage your audience to engage in conversations and share your posts.

- Use Facebook Live: Live videos tend to rank higher in the newsfeed because they generate more engagement. Use this feature to connect with your audience in real-time.

- Focus on Groups: Facebook has been shifting its focus towards Groups, where engagement is often higher. Participate in relevant groups and share content that adds value to the community.

2. Instagram

- Leverage Instagram Stories and Reels: Instagram's algorithm favors Reels and Stories due to their high engagement rates. Use these features to increase visibility.

- Optimize for Save and Share: Content that users save or share with others signals high value to the algorithm. Create content that your audience will want to revisit or share.

- Hashtags and Keywords: Use relevant hashtags and keywords to reach a broader audience. Instagram allows up to 30 hashtags per post, so research and use the ones that are most relevant to your content.

3. Twitter

- Engage in Real-Time: Twitter's algorithm values timeliness, so posting during peak hours when your audience is active can boost your reach. Use tools like Twitter Analytics to determine the best times to tweet.

- Retweets and Replies: Engaging with others through retweets and replies can increase your visibility. The algorithm favors content that generates conversations.

- Use Trends to Your Advantage: Participating in trending conversations or using trending hashtags can help your tweets gain traction. However, ensure your content is relevant to the trend.

4. TikTok

- Hook Users Quickly: TikTok's algorithm heavily weighs the first few seconds of a video. Capture attention immediately to increase watch time, which is a significant ranking factor.

- Use Trending Sounds and Effects: Incorporating popular sounds, effects, or challenges into your videos can help you reach a wider audience.

- Post Frequently: TikTok favors active users. Posting regularly increases your chances of being discovered by new followers.

Tips to Maximize Your Social Media Reach

NOW THAT YOU UNDERSTAND the basics of how social media algorithms work, here are some actionable tips to help you optimize your content strategy:

1. Create Engaging Content: Focus on creating content that resonates with your audience and encourages interaction. Ask questions, host polls, or prompt your audience to comment on your posts.

2. Post Consistently: Maintain a regular posting schedule. Consistency signals to algorithms that your profile is active and worth promoting.

3. Analyze and Adapt: Use analytics tools provided by each platform to monitor your performance. Pay attention to which types of content perform best and adapt your strategy accordingly.

4. Optimize for Mobile: Most users access social media via mobile devices, so ensure your content is mobile-friendly. Vertical videos, for example, perform better on mobile platforms like TikTok and Instagram.

5. Collaborate with Others: Partnering with other creators or influencers can help you reach a broader audience. Cross-promotions and collaborations can significantly boost your visibility.

6. Engage with Your Audience: Respond to comments, engage with your followers' content, and be active in relevant communities. Building relationships can increase your content's reach.

7. Stay Updated on Algorithm Changes: Social media platforms frequently update their algorithms. Stay informed about these changes by following platform blogs, social media news, and industry influencers.

Conclusion

UNDERSTANDING SOCIAL media algorithms is key to maximizing your reach and building a successful online presence. While algorithms can seem complex, they all share a common goal of promoting content that is engaging, relevant, and timely. By tailoring your content strategy to align with these factors, you can improve your visibility, connect with your audience more effectively, and achieve your social media goals. Remember, success on social media isn't just about following trends—it's about creating content that genuinely resonates with your audience and adds value to their experience.

Expand Your Email Subscriber List Cost-Free

In today's digital landscape, growing your email subscriber list is a crucial aspect of building a successful online presence. While paid advertising can be effective, there are creative ways to *"Expand Your Email Subscriber List Cost-Free."* Let's explore five innovative strategies that can help you increase your email subscribers without spending a dime.

1. Utilizing Social Media Platforms Effectively

SOCIAL MEDIA PLATFORMS are a powerful tool for reaching a wide audience and attracting potential subscribers. By creating engaging and shareable content, you can drive traffic to your website and encourage visitors to subscribe to your email list. Consider running contests or giveaways that require participants to sign up for your newsletter, leveraging the viral nature of social media to grow your subscriber base.

2. Creating Engaging Lead Magnets

A LEAD MAGNET IS AN incentive offered to potential subscribers in exchange for their email address. By developing high-quality and valuable lead magnets such as e-books, checklists, or exclusive content, you can entice visitors to subscribe to your email list. Make sure your lead magnets are relevant to your target audience's needs and interests to maximize sign-up rates and build a loyal subscriber base.

3. Leveraging Partnerships for Cross-Promotion

COLLABORATING WITH like-minded businesses or influencers can significantly expand your reach and attract new subscribers. Seek out partnerships for cross-promotion opportunities, such as guest blogging on each other's websites or co-hosting webinars or events. By tapping into each other's audiences, you can introduce your brand to a wider demographic and drive more subscribers to your email list.

4. Optimizing Your Website for Conversions

YOUR WEBSITE PLAYS a crucial role in converting visitors into email subscribers. Ensure that your website is user-friendly, visually appealing, and optimized for conversions. Use clear call-to-action buttons and strategically-placed sign-up forms to capture visitors' attention and encourage them to subscribe. Implementing exit-intent pop-ups or offering exclusive discounts to new subscribers can also improve your conversion rates.

5. Engaging with Your Email Subscribers

BUILDING A STRONG RELATIONSHIP with your email subscribers is essential for maintaining a healthy and engaged subscriber list. Send personalized and valuable content to your subscribers regularly, such as newsletters, blog updates, or special promotions. Encourage two-way communication by inviting feedback, conducting surveys, or hosting exclusive Q&A sessions to foster a sense of community and loyalty among your subscribers.

By implementing these creative strategies, you can effectively grow your email subscriber list organically and expand your online reach without incurring additional costs. Remember, consistency, relevance, and value are key to attracting and retaining subscribers in the competitive digital landscape. Start applying these tactics today and watch your email list flourish!

Remember, email marketing remains a powerful tool for driving engagement and conversions, so make sure you leverage these strategies to unlock the full potential of your email subscriber list!

Uncover 7 Free Strategies to Boost Website Traffic

In the digital realm where visibility is key, driving organic traffic to your website without breaking the bank can seem like an elusive goal. But fear not! There are effective strategies that can pave the way for a surge in website visits and clicks without relying on costly ads or buying views. Today, we unveil the seven hidden gems that will propel your online presence to new heights. Strategies to boost website traffic:

1. Master SEO Magic

SEARCH ENGINE OPTIMIZATION (SEO) is your trusty sidekick in the quest for increased traffic. By optimizing your content with relevant keywords, meta descriptions, and titles, you can enhance your website's visibility in search engine results, attracting organic traffic like bees to honey.

2. Craft Compelling Content

CONTENT IS KING, AND quality content reigns supreme. Engage your audience with valuable, informative, and entertaining content that keeps them coming back for more. Whether it's blog posts, videos, or infographics, compelling content is the magnet that draws visitors to your site.

3. Embrace the Power of Social Media

LEVERAGE THE VAST REACH of social media platforms to promote your website and drive traffic. Engage with your audience, share your content, and join relevant communities to widen your online presence. A strong social media strategy can create a ripple effect that leads users straight to your website.

4. Harness the Potential of Email Marketing

CREATE AN EMAIL MARKETING campaign to connect directly with your audience. Share updates, promotions, and exclusive content to entice subscribers to visit your website. A well-crafted email can spark curiosity and drive traffic organically.

5. Network and Collaborate

BUILD PARTNERSHIPS and collaborate with influencers, bloggers, or other websites in your niche. Guest posting, cross-promotions, or shoutouts can introduce your website to new audiences and drive traffic through mutual support and shared exposure.

6. Optimize User Experience

A SEAMLESS USER EXPERIENCE is crucial for retaining visitors and encouraging them to explore your website further. Make sure your site is easy to navigate, visually appealing, and mobile-friendly. A positive user experience can keep visitors engaged and increase the likelihood of return visits.

7. Engage with Your Audience

INTERACT WITH YOUR audience through comments, forums, or live chats. By fostering a sense of community and addressing their concerns, you can build trust and loyalty. Engaged users are more likely to share your content, leading to increased visibility and organic traffic.

Now armed with these hidden strategies, you have the tools to propel your website to new heights without spending a dime on ads. By embracing SEO, creating compelling content, utilizing social media, and fostering user engagement, you can drive organic traffic and clicks, establishing your website as a go-to destination in the digital landscape.

Remember, the journey to increased website traffic is a marathon, not a sprint. Stay consistent, track your progress, and adapt your strategies to best suit your audience. With patience, perseverance, and these hidden gems in your arsenal, your website is poised for success in the competitive online arena.

Website Loading Woes: Speed Optimization for Musicians

In today's fast-paced digital world, your website is often the first impression you make on potential fans, collaborators, and industry professionals. A slow-loading site can turn visitors away before they even get a chance to hear your music or learn about your upcoming shows. Speed optimization for musicians isn't just a technical concern; it's a crucial part of building and maintaining an effective online presence. In this post, we'll explore practical tips to optimize your website's loading times and ensure a smooth, fast experience for your visitors.

1. Choose the Right Hosting Provider

YOUR WEBSITE'S PERFORMANCE starts with your hosting provider. A reliable and fast web host is essential for quick loading times.

- Shared vs. Dedicated Hosting: While shared hosting is cheaper, it often results in slower load times due to the number of sites sharing the same server. If you can afford it, consider upgrading to a dedicated hosting plan or a Virtual Private Server (VPS) for better performance.

- Content Delivery Network (CDN): A CDN stores copies of your site's content on servers around the world, delivering it to users from the nearest server. This reduces the distance data has to travel and speeds up loading times for your global audience.

2. Optimize Your Images

IMAGES ARE OFTEN THE largest files on a website, and unoptimized images can significantly slow down your site.

- Use the Right File Format: JPEGs are great for photographs, while PNGs are better for images that require transparency. Avoid using BMPs or TIFFs, as they are not web-friendly.

- Compress Images: Use image compression tools like TinyPNG, JPEGmini, or Photoshop's "Save for Web" option to reduce file sizes without sacrificing quality. This can drastically reduce load times.

- Lazy Loading: Implement lazy loading, a technique where images load only when they're about to enter the user's view. This reduces the initial load time and improves the user experience.

3. Minimize HTTP Requests

EVERY ELEMENT ON YOUR web page—images, scripts, stylesheets—requires an HTTP request. The more requests, the slower your site.

- Combine Files: Combine multiple CSS files into one and do the same for JavaScript files. This reduces the number of requests and speeds up load times.

- Use CSS Sprites: CSS sprites allow you to combine multiple images into a single file. The browser then loads the single file and displays the correct image portion. This is especially useful for icons and buttons.

- Reduce Plugins: If you're using a platform like WordPress, minimize the number of plugins. Each plugin adds to the number of HTTP requests, so only use the ones that are essential.

4. Enable Browser Caching

BROWSER CACHING ALLOWS your site to store files on a visitor's device, so they don't have to be downloaded every time the user visits your site.

- Set Expiry Dates: By setting expiry dates on cached content, you can control how long files are stored on the user's device. Use tools like YSlow or Google PageSpeed Insights to identify which files should be cached.

- Leverage .htaccess: If you have access to your site's .htaccess file, you can manually enable caching and set expiry dates for different types of content.

5. Minify CSS, JavaScript, and HTML

MINIFICATION IS THE process of removing unnecessary characters (like spaces and line breaks) from your code, making it smaller and faster to load.

- Use Online Tools: Tools like UglifyJS for JavaScript, CSSNano for CSS, and HTMLMinifier for HTML can help you minify your files.

- Automate the Process: If you're using a build tool like Gulp or Webpack, you can automate minification during your site's build process, ensuring your files are always optimized.

6. Optimize Your Music Player

IF YOUR SITE FEATURES a music player, it's important to ensure it doesn't slow down your site.

- Use Streaming Services: Instead of hosting large audio files on your server, embed music from streaming platforms like SoundCloud, Spotify, or Bandcamp. These platforms are optimized for fast loading and offer high-quality streaming.

- Optimize Embedded Players: If you're embedding a music player, make sure it loads asynchronously, meaning it won't hold up the rest of your site's content from loading.

7. Enable Gzip Compression

GZIP COMPRESSION REDUCES the size of your files before they are sent to the browser, which can significantly decrease loading times.
- Activate Gzip: Most web servers, including Apache and Nginx, support Gzip compression. You can enable it through your site's .htaccess file or via your server's configuration settings.
- Check Compression: Use online tools like Gtmetrix or Google PageSpeed Insights to check if Gzip compression is enabled on your site and see the difference in file sizes.

8. Use a Lightweight Theme

IF YOU'RE USING A CONTENT management system (CMS) like WordPress, the theme you choose can greatly impact your site's speed.
- Choose a Fast Theme: Opt for themes that are built with performance in mind. Avoid overly complex themes with excessive animations, sliders, and widgets that can slow down your site.
- Custom vs. Premade Themes: If you have the budget, consider a custom-built theme that's optimized for your specific needs. Otherwise, choose a well-coded, lightweight premade theme and customize it to suit your style.

9. Monitor Your Website's Performance

REGULARLY MONITORING your website's performance helps you identify issues and make necessary adjustments.
- Use Speed Testing Tools: Tools like Google PageSpeed Insights, Pingdom, and Gtmetrix provide detailed reports on your site's speed and offer suggestions for improvement.

- Analyze Traffic Spikes: If you experience slowdowns during traffic spikes, consider using a service like Cloudflare to manage the increased load or upgrading your hosting plan to handle more visitors.

10. Keep Your Site Updated

KEEPING YOUR SITE'S software up-to-date is crucial for both security and performance.
- Update CMS and Plugins: Regularly update your CMS, plugins, and themes to ensure they're optimized and free from vulnerabilities that could slow down your site.
- Remove Unused Plugins and Themes: Deactivate and delete any plugins or themes you're not using. Even inactive plugins can slow down your site, so keep your installation clean.

Conclusion

OPTIMIZING YOUR WEBSITE'S loading times is essential for keeping your audience engaged and improving your overall online presence. With the right strategies, you can ensure that your site is fast, efficient, and provides a great user experience, even if you're working with limited resources. By choosing the right hosting, optimizing your images, minimizing HTTP requests, and staying on top of updates, you can create a site that not only looks great but also performs at its best. Remember, in the digital age, speed is not just a luxury—it's a necessity.

DIY Music Videos: Solving Lighting and Filming Challenges

Creating a music video is a powerful way to visually express your music and connect with your audience. However, if you're an independent artist, budget constraints can make producing a professional-looking video seem daunting. The good news is that you don't need expensive gear or a big crew to create a compelling music video. With some creativity and a few practical tips, you can solve common lighting and filming challenges to produce a video that looks polished and professional. Here's how.

1. Plan Your Video Concept Carefully

BEFORE DIVING INTO filming, it's essential to plan your video concept. A well-thought-out plan will help you make the most of your resources and avoid unnecessary expenses.

- Storyboarding: Sketch out your ideas in a storyboard. This doesn't have to be artistically perfect—just a simple outline of scenes and shots will do. Storyboarding helps you visualize the flow of the video and ensures you capture all the necessary footage.

- Location Scouting: Look for locations that align with your video's theme. Public spaces, parks, and even your home can serve as excellent settings. Consider the natural lighting available in these locations, as it can save you time and money on lighting setups.

- Keep It Simple: Don't overcomplicate your concept. A straightforward idea executed well can be far more impactful than an elaborate one that stretches your resources thin.

2. Use Natural Light to Your Advantage

LIGHTING IS ONE OF the most critical elements in video production. While professional lighting setups can be expensive, you can achieve great results by harnessing natural light.
  - Golden Hour: The golden hour, shortly after sunrise or before sunset, provides soft, warm light that is flattering for video. Plan your shoot around these times to make the most of this natural lighting.
  - Cloudy Days: Overcast days offer diffused, even lighting that eliminates harsh shadows. This is ideal for outdoor shoots, as it provides consistent lighting without the need for reflectors or additional equipment.
  - Window Light: For indoor shoots, position your subject near a large window to take advantage of natural light. Use sheer curtains to diffuse the light if it's too harsh.

3. DIY Lighting Solutions

IF YOU NEED ADDITIONAL lighting, there are several budget-friendly options you can create yourself.
  - Reflectors: A simple reflector can bounce light onto your subject, filling in shadows and creating a more even look. You can make your own reflector using a piece of white foam board or aluminum foil.
  - Household Lamps: Standard lamps can serve as effective lighting tools. Use lampshades to diffuse the light, or bounce the light off walls or ceilings for a softer effect. Experiment with different bulbs to achieve the color temperature you want.
  - LED Light Panels: Affordable LED light panels can provide consistent, adjustable light for your shoot. They're portable, easy to set up, and can be powered by batteries, making them perfect for on-the-go filming.

4. Stabilize Your Shots

SHAKY FOOTAGE CAN MAKE even the best-planned video look amateurish. Stabilizing your shots is essential for creating a professional-looking video.

- Tripod: Invest in a good tripod for steady, stable shots. There are many affordable options available that are lightweight and easy to use.
- DIY Stabilizers: If you don't have a tripod, try using a stack of books, a sturdy table, or even a pile of blankets to stabilize your camera.
- Handheld Techniques: If you're shooting handheld, use both hands to hold the camera, keep your elbows close to your body, and move smoothly. You can also use the camera's in-built stabilization features if available.

5. Use Your Smartphone Effectively

MODERN SMARTPHONES come equipped with powerful cameras that are more than capable of shooting high-quality video.

- Manual Settings: Explore your phone's camera settings and experiment with manual controls like ISO, shutter speed, and focus. This allows you to have more control over the final look of your video.
- External Lenses: Consider investing in external lenses designed for smartphones. These lenses can give you a wider field of view, a sharper image, or even macro capabilities, expanding your creative options.
- Filmic Apps: Use apps like Filmic Pro to gain more control over your phone's camera settings. These apps often include features like manual focus, exposure controls, and color grading tools.

6. Focus on Composition

GOOD COMPOSITION CAN elevate your video and make it look more professional, even if you're working with basic equipment.

- Rule of Thirds: Divide your frame into thirds, both horizontally and vertically, and place your subject along these lines or at their intersections. This creates a balanced and visually appealing shot.

- Leading Lines: Use natural lines in your environment, such as roads, fences, or pathways, to draw the viewer's eye towards your subject.

- Depth of Field: Create depth in your shots by including elements in the foreground, middle ground, and background. This adds a sense of dimension and makes your video more engaging.

7. Edit with Care

EDITING IS WHERE YOUR footage comes together to create the final product. Even if you're editing on a budget, you can achieve professional results with careful attention to detail.

- Free Editing Software: Programs like DaVinci Resolve, HitFilm Express, and iMovie offer powerful editing tools at no cost. These tools provide a range of features for cutting, color grading, and adding effects to your video.

- Color Grading: Color grading can significantly enhance the look of your video. Use it to correct any lighting inconsistencies and to create a cohesive visual style.

- Keep It Simple: Don't overdo it with transitions and effects. Simple cuts and subtle transitions are often more effective than flashy effects that can distract from the music and visuals.

8. Test and Adjust

BEFORE THE ACTUAL SHOOT, it's a good idea to do a test run. This allows you to troubleshoot any issues and make adjustments before you start filming.

- Lighting Test: Set up your lighting and film a short test clip. Review the footage to ensure the lighting is consistent and flattering.

- Sound Check: If your video includes live sound or dialogue, do a sound check to ensure clarity and minimize background noise. Consider using an external microphone for better audio quality.

- Rehearsal: Run through your scenes or performance to get comfortable with the camera and the space. This will make the actual shoot smoother and more efficient.

Conclusion

CREATING A PROFESSIONAL-looking music video on a budget is entirely possible with the right approach and a bit of creativity. By planning carefully, making the most of natural light, using DIY lighting solutions, and paying attention to composition and editing, you can overcome common filming challenges and produce a video that truly represents your music.

<u>**Remember, the key to a great music video is not how much money you spend, but how effectively you use the resources you have.**</u>

With these tips in hand, you're well on your way to creating a visually compelling and polished music video, even on a shoestring budget.

Also by Neil J Milliner

Artful Investments: Enhancing Your Property Value Through Fine Art

E-commerce SEO Strategies: Selling Online Successfully

Fast Track Your Songwriting Career-Essential Tips and Hints to Master Your Craft and Build a Lasting Career

The Ultimate Singer's Guide-Practical Tips to Improve Your Voice and Achieve Your Vocal Dreams

Branding & Networking Success for Bands

Mastering Fan Engagement-Pro-Level Hints to Create Authentic Connections and Build Loyalty

Mastering Live Performance & Touring-Pro Level Tips and Hints to Elevate Your Stage Presence and Tour Like a Pro

Music Production Mastery-Step-by-Step Tutorials to Fast-Track Your Way to Professional Success

The Musician's Tech Toolbox-Essential Technical Tips and Equipment Know-How for Musicians

The Ultimate Musician's Website Guide-Step-by-Step Tutorials to Engage Fans and Showcase Your Talent

Milton Keynes UK
Ingram Content Group UK Ltd.
UKHW042002281024
450365UK00003B/109